Africa's Refugee Crisis

This English translation could never have been undertaken without the financial help offered by two British NGOs, CAFOD (Catholic Action For Overseas Development) and Christian Aid, and that forthcoming from the World Council of Churches. We hereby ask these organizations to accept our heartfelt gratitude.

Africa's Refugee Crisis

What's To Be Done?

CIMADE, INODEP, MINK

Translated by Michael John

Zed Books Ltd.

Africa's Refugee Crisis was originally published in French by Editions L'Harmattan, 7 Rue de l'Ecole-Polytechnique, 75005 Paris, in 1984; first published in English in an updated edition by Zed Books Ltd., 57 Caledonian Road, London N1 9BU, in 1986.

Cover photo by M. Kobayashi
Printed by The Bath Press, Avon.

British Library Cataloguing in Publication Data

Africa's refugee crisis : what's to be done.
  1. Refugees—Africa
  I. CIMADE   II. INODEP   III. MINK   IV. Afrique,
  terre des refugiés. *English*
  325'.21'096   HV640.5.A/

  ISBN 0-86232-469-6
  ISBN 0-86232-470-X Pbk

US Distributor
Biblio Distribution Center, 81 Adams Drive,
Totowa, New Jersey 07512, USA.

Contents

Tables

This book is dedicated to the millions of African refugees, in the hope that the years to come will bring an end to their sufferings.

CIMADE, 176 rue de Grenelle, 75007 Paris, France.
INODEP, 49 rue de la Glacière, 75013 Paris, France.
MINK, B.P. 46, 94202 Ivry-sur-Seine, Cedex, France.

Preface

When refugees from Czechoslovakia or Chile are asked what we can do to help them, they all reply: 'Talk about our country. Don't let people forget us!'

They know that the best protection for oppressed peoples is the pressure of public opinion. And indeed this has a greater influence than we think on the decisions made by certain governments. It brings what they do into the limelight.

The peoples we have just named enjoy a partial protection in this way. And one or the other class of refugees are brought to the front page of the world news by regular information, given time and again. But a certain type of publicity, often used in a political way, would have us think that the only refugees are those of which we hear the most. In this way the dramatic problem of the refugees in Africa remains unknown to most people.

CIMADE, INODEP and the International N'Krumah Movement have deservedly done their best to lift the veil (or should we say: break the hermetic seal?) behind which this tragedy lies hidden. They have undertaken serious analyses, collected evidence of high quality, and done research into the root causes of an evil which affects five million human beings. Thanks to their principle that no information should be given which has not been thoroughly verified, the texts we are publishing here constitute a very reliable working tool.

May they also serve the peoples of whom they speak, bringing them immediate relief and, with the passage of time, contributing to their freedom. In this way they will bring forth the fruits of a much needed hope.

'Talk about us': that is what we have done.

'Don't let them forget us': from now on, we are all responsible!

Daniel Mayer
Former President of the
International Federation of
Human Rights

1

Introduction

The articles and the various contributions which make up this dossier should be seen from the same angle as the research which gave rise to them, if they are to be understood and their limits to be seen. The tragedy of African refugees in Africa itself is as yet uninterrupted. If we are to fight against it effectively, much more is to be said — and even more to be done.

During the winter of 1981–82, CIMADE and INODEP organized two seminars, researching into the causes of this tragedy. They were helped by a number of militant Africans living in France, often with the legal status of refugees. We discovered with astonishment the vast public ignorance, in France and in Europe at large, concerning the numbers and whereabouts of refugee groups in Africa. The media rightly use all their influence to sensitize the international conscience on similar movements of the population of Southeast Asia, and indeed the 'boat people' are entering Europe and the United States in large numbers. Is it because the greater number of African refugees who leave their country or their tribal area remain in the same continent that public opinion is unaware of the gravity of their situation? Is it because more Asians than Africans are in flight from countries or regimes known as 'communist' that the media of the so-called 'free world' tell us more about their misfortunes?

The UN declared 1982 to be a year of sensitization and international mobilization in favour of refugees. Our two seminars proposed a double objective:

1. To find out exactly what is happening. True figures and accurate descriptions were taken from the most trustworthy statistics and sources of information.
2. To analyse the causes, immediate or remote, recent or rooted in past events, of the constant development of the stream of refugees in Africa.

These two seminars produced a small working document, which is developed in this dossier. At the end of this first stage we felt that we should pursue the work with greater means. Completing the information and the statistics proved a fairly easy job, but it was more delicate to make the analysis. To avoid ideological slogans on the one hand, and expressions full of commiseration on the other, we needed to meet 'resource persons' from the field, refugees themselves, or those responsible at one level or another for the future of the refugees. These witnesses became more and more necessary as we discovered the determining importance of the political dimension of the problem.

And this is not only true from the point of view of those who took part in the seminars. We can give a simple example, without attaching any special importance to it: Professor Eya Nchema, a member of the opposition from Equatorial Guinea, addressed the Subcommission on Human Rights in the Palais des Nations in Geneva in August 1982 on behalf of the International Movement for Brotherly Union between Races and Peoples (MIUFRP). He established a link, which in his eyes was clear, between the alarming number of refugees in Africa and the violation of human rights on this continent.

Today we deplore more than 5,000,000 refugees in Africa, whereas at the end of the 1950s there were no more than 200,000. In 1970 the number had grown to 750,000 and by 1973 there were already 1,000,000. In 1979, 4,000,000 could be counted. According to the MIUFRP, there is a danger that before the end of this century the figure will be between 15 million and 20 million.

For Professor Nchema 'it is true that many things which happen in Africa today are to be traced to past colonialism and present-day military intervention. But why does the international community draw a veil of silence over the massacres which take place daily on the African continent?' The responsibility is to be attributed to 'the many African leaders who have no regard for the most elementary Human Rights of their peoples'. It would cost certain African states less to attempt to reconcile their citizens than to pay mercenaries to bolster up the oligarchies which presently hold power.

To know if a government practises state terrorism, it is only necessary to count the number of people who prefer to live in exile during its term of office. The representative of the MIUFRP holds that the majority of the African refugees come from countries which are members of the OAU. It is high time that the UN faced up to its responsibility towards all peoples living under 'tyrannical' regimes, and encouraged the struggle undertaken throughout Africa against the violation of human rights, for 'it is beyond question that the struggle against the oligarchies in Africa is a way to alleviate the tragedy of African refugees' (*Le Monde*, 28 August 1982).

The last few pages give a rapid survey of the development of the situation which led us to organize in Paris, on 6 November 1982, an international day of reflection and mobilization in favour of the African refugees in Africa.

To convoke and organize this meeting, CIMADE and INODEP were joined by the International N'Krumah Movement (MINK), which is based in Paris, and the International Association 'Education and Liberation' (Geneva). The Committee of Sponsors was headed by Mr Daniel Mayer, at the time President of the International Federation of Human Rights, and author of the preface to this book. He was seconded by: Mr Guy Aurenche, barrister-at-law; Mr Philippe Farine, member of International Solidarities; Mr Joseph Ki-Zerbo, representing the Centre of Studies for African Development; Mr Edgard Pisani, of the Commission of the European Community; and Mr Georges Tsetsis, of the World Council of Churches.

During the preparatory meetings we decided, for practical reasons, to limit our investigations to the refugees living in three regions, chosen for the reasons we explain below: the 'Horn' of Africa, the sector constituted by the Zaire, Angola, Rwanda and Burundi, and Southern Africa. Thanks to the support of both governmental and non-governmental organizations,[1] we were able to call in 'resource-persons' from these areas and the information they brought us and the analyses they offered were of considerable help[2] in our discussions.

For reasons easy to understand, those who took part in this international day had been invited by the intermediary of militant movements. The closing session alone was open to a wider public, and representatives of the press and the radio were invited and received copies of the final declaration.[3]

Among the motions taken by the participants (about 180 in number) was the desire to see this international day followed up by action in the field, especially on the level of education. They also asked that an effort be made to develop information about African refugees and to popularize analyses of the situation. If this is not done, other actions are likely to be of little avail, if we except the programmes of emergency aid run by specialized organizations and institutions.

That is why those who were behind the day of reflection on 6 November have often met since. This book is the outcome of their work.

As we were finishing the French version of it, serious events were taking place in Chad which were to arouse tribal rivalries once again and oppose the interests of Libya, France and the United States, while in Southern Africa the RSA, with the help of America, was to succeed in bringing Mozambique to her knees, and even Angola. The number of refugees was to go on growing and their misfortunes to increase.

Before making the difficult but necessary attempt to clarify the meaning of the term 'refugee', and discussing the consequences that this conception has in international law, we think it is important to paint a general picture of the situation on the historical and statistical levels. Population transfers have long existed in Africa. They have had many causes, among which the search for a political refuge is but one.

The history of Africa is still very little known, at least by most people. But an increasing number of studies, often supported by oral evidence, bear witness to the fact that, long before the penetration of European colonial powers, a large number of peoples in different parts of the continent had been obliged to take to exile amidst great suffering. The colonial powers tried to 'stabilize' certain native populations to suit their economic or political interests, even when their living conditions were driving them to seek refuge elsewhere. Peoples were often obliged, on the other hand, to leave their homelands in order to swell the construction sites and plantations of their new masters. The accession of most of the former colonies to independence round about 1960, and the new forms of domination which have developed since then and which are confronting one another in Africa, were to engender movements of depopulation and the search for sanctuary of a new type.

That is what the first part of this dossier wishes briefly to summarize. We have deliberately reduced descriptions of these groups to a minimum, especially accounts of the material and moral conditions in which the flights take place, the 'provisional' installation in camps, the proportion of those who die, the food and medicine sent out to help but which end up being stored and left to rot . . . All these scourges are already well known or can at least be easily discovered. Would upsetting and horrifying descriptions of them increase our pity and stimulate our generosity? Alas, nothing is less certain. We believe it is more important to discover the causes and establish the responsibilities, in order to provide mobilization and militant commitment with a firm basis on the level at which the seeking for sanctuary comes into being and is developed.

The three other sections of our dossier are going to attempt this type of analysis of the situation that faces us today.

The responsibility of African governments and governmental organizations is evident. First on the level of each state: the violation of human rights, ethnic and/or religious conflicts and tensions. But also on the level of the relations between states, and even of the contradictions which exist in the operation of the OAU. We shall return to this point. But a deeper and more painstaking analysis reveals the importance of factors which are exterior to the African continent. If this continent had not in recent times become one of the stakes in world geo-political and economic strategies, the point where the great powers confront one another, the fate of the refugees and their number would be quite different.

That is why the second part of this dossier starts from the causes and responsibilities which lie outside of Africa. On this point, our analyses are still limited and insufficient.

Insufficient, because we have not had sufficient time to study the influence of the economic policies of multinational firms. INODEP has already shown, in former studies, that these firms are not, in the true sense of the word, 'supra-' or 'multi-' national economic forces because, generally speaking, the greater part (absolute or relative) of their capital is in the hands of the citizens of one country. Nevertheless they dispose of a power of decision which is largely autonomous with respect to the governments of the great powers. Thousands of workers depend on these decisions for their living wage, in slums, in mining camps and in the country. At a moment's notice, they may find themselves obliged to seek refuge elsewhere if they wish to survive.

Limited, because if the influence of America, the USSR, Cuba and France is determining, we need to do a fuller analysis:

1: of the role of Israel. Like France at the present time, Israel is linked with American strategy, but still disposes of a certain freedom of action.

2: of the place held by the People's Republic of China. China has maintained a presence in Africa since the end of the 1950s, but she works quietly and so is little known. Chinese policy in Africa was at first based on the principle of supporting movements fighting for freedom, but it quickly became one of the pivots of the struggle for influence between China and the USSR. In many countries such as Zimbabwe or Namibia, China has simply backed the movement which is in opposition to that supported by Moscow. This policy has led China to work closely with the governments and intelligence services of France, Great Britain and America.

3: of the growing influence to be attributed to the forces of Islam, despite their internal divisions which are maintained by the great powers.

It is nevertheless a fact that the tensions, conflicts and wars which ravage Africa and are thus one of the main causes of the flow of refugees are deeply rooted, both to the north and south of the Sahara, in the economic, political and ideological rivalries of powers outside the African continent. Our dossier reminds us that we should evaluate the causes and responsibilities of African governments towards the refugees in the light of this situation.

But we must look beyond these causes and responsibilities which are both exterior to Africa and within the continent. They may be determining, but they are none the less of a general nature. The third part of the dossier will attempt to determine the causes and responsibilities which are specific to the regions to which we have decided to give special attention: the Horn, parts of Central Africa and Southern Africa.

A simple glance at the statistics determined this choice. These are the regions in which the tragedy of the refugees appears most dramatically, whether we consider their numbers, their present living conditions, or the situation which decided them to leave home.

But there were two other reasons. One of the main causes of the flow of refugees is to be seen clearly in each of these areas: war in the Horn, apartheid in South Africa, and in between, in a region which is economically rich and strategically decisive, economic and political oppression by the black bourgeoisies which relay international imperialism. Secondly, the failure of the international definitions of a 'refugee' to face up to the analysis of the movements of the populations in these specific regions. They appear superficial and irrelevant, because the concept of a 'refugee' lacks precision, depth and pungency, as we shall try to show at the end of this dossier. The current definitions give too much importance to 'established order' and to 'natural' calamities, and prove unable to meet a serious ideological criticism. Indeed, our dossier says practically nothing about natural calamities, and this omission must be explained.

Take the case of the droughts which ravage the region of the Sahel and the sector in the south of the Horn. They have been known to the public on a large scale through the media since 1973. Ruined famers and stock-breeders flee in their thousands, seeking refuge in the south, where water is more abundant. But long before this date, equally severe droughts have hit these same regions. The colonial administrations, especially in Mali, Burkina-Faso (then Upper Volta) and Niger, had studied this 'natural' cyclic calamity and noted (with a precision remarkable for the time) the monthly rainfall and the strength of the rivers in each district.

There is no doubt that the increase in population and livestock has created a greater need for water. But in the same regions, and despite these droughts, neither the area cultivated nor the harvest of exported crops have on average diminished. Indeed from Senegal to Chad, the tendency is rather to note an increase. What plans, regularly pursued at the expense of cultures of sustenance, are responsible for the deforestation and the wastage of the water-pockets in the subsoil? Who is it who provides thousands of peasants with such precarious ecological conditions that a drought more serious than usual can turn them into fleeing hordes, dying of hunger? And why was no provision made for such a drought, which can often be foreseen?

Another 'natural' calamity which is often evoked as an explanation is the desertification of the soil, principally by erosion and lateritization. But it is astonishing to find this still considered as a valid explanation of the refugee movements, since René Dumont has clearly shown that these catastrophes can be anticipated and arrested.

Lack of water? lack of fertility? growth of the population? All these factors exist. But in the recent dossier of the organization 'Brothers of Mankind' (*Frères des Hommes*), entitled *The Rights of Peoples to Feed Themselves*, balanced and competent answers are given to the questions we have just asked.

Most frequently 'natural' calamities only strike people because those who are responsible have taken risks or, more serious still, have treated whole social groups with disdain, considering their survival a matter of less importance than the development of financial profits, the sale of luxury goods, and the investment of ill-gotten capital in foreign banks.

Many other regions of Africa are concerned with the problem of refugees. Some countries, like South Africa, oblige populations to leave their ethnic territories for another location without expelling them from the country. The reasons are different in each case. Often, as in the central zone, countries force their own citizens to seek refuge outside the country and, at the same time, accept the entry of people from neighbouring states. Many descriptions can be given of the situation and they correspond to the complex situations of the different types of refugee. And how should we describe the families and the tribes whose rights are encroached on more and more and whose resources and security get less and less every year, but who are unable to move because their calls for help find no echo in the international conscience? The territories occupied by the state of Israel are not the only places where indigenous populations (like the Palestinians) are refugees on their own lands and in their own cultural environment.

Before closing this dossier we have tried to plead for a better definition of the term 'refugee', which will take account of cases like these. This will help the international community to make more effective commitments in favour of refugees.

At the end we give the texts of the resolutions and proposals voted at the end of this international study day (6 November 1982), and add a new chapter on the International Conference on African Refugees in Africa (ICARA II) which was held in Geneva on 9–11 July 1984 (see Chapter 15 below).

The general conclusion is drawn by Mr Melaku Kifle, who is responsible for African refugees at the World Council of Churches.

Notes

1. Especially the French Ministry for Cooperation, and the World Council of Churches.

2. We are very sorry we cannot give their names in this book. But we wish them to know how deep is our gratitude.

3. This declaration will be found on pp. 121–2.

Part 1:
Peoples in Exile

1. A Little History

Africa is a huge territory, geographically vulnerable, underpopulated but possessing immense natural and mining resources. It has been constantly submitted to political, economic and social domination, and this has led to political and social de-structuring. As a result, there are more refugees in Africa than in any other continent of our planet.

One African out of a hundred is today a refugee, and this figure is certainly an underestimate if we consider the multiplicity of expulsions like those from Nigeria (2 millions) in February 1983 or from Uganda, and the depopulation or forced migration of the populations of Ethiopia, Zimbabwe, Mozambique, Angola and Namibia, fleeing colonial or civil wars, or driven to move by famine. Then again we must take into account the savage repression exercised by the army or the police of the apartheid regime in Southern Africa against the Blacks and the patriots of South Africa and Namibia.

Of course there is a tendency, when you look at the facts, to consider that the causes and the results of the phenomenon are inevitable. Our observations show that this is not true. A process continuous since ancient times, and known in more recent periods of history as the slave trade or direct colonization, has obliged the African peoples, from the north to the south, to flee from acts of pillage, commercial vandalism and military occupation. Add to this the natural cataclysms which tragically brought in their wake diseases and emigration.

In Antiquity

The Phoenicians and the Assyrians seem to have been the first to open the way. Their armies occupied the north-east of Africa (Egypt) and all the north and systematically pillaged the populations and the regions they discovered.

From time to time the Egyptian populations of the Nile delta were obliged to take refuge in the south; the inhabitants of north Africa withdrew into the Atlas mountains or the oases of the Sahara.

● The Phoenician merchants settled at Carthage, where they set up a trading centre covering the Mediterranean and Atlantic zones. They hired mercenary seamen to scour the African coasts of the Atlantic in search of gold, ivory, animals, spices and, above all, slaves.

● The most renowned among these navigators was Amon the Carthaginian, who was famous for his legendary and barbarous cruelty. Wherever he plundered, he left nothing. He lived 1,000 years before Christ.

● The Assyrians did as much on the eastern coasts of Africa.

● The rise of Roman imperialism brought new rivals; Rome became the ally of the Africans of Mauretania and chased the Phoenicians out of Africa.

● The Phoenicians regularly plundered the east coast of Africa and sought to procure black slaves for the kingdoms of the Middle East. This went on right up to the Middle Ages.

● We can affirm that this was a major cause of the constitution by the Africans of large empires before, during and after the Middle Ages. Among these we can name the empires of Bafour, Ghana, Aksoum, Benin, Monomotapa, Ethiopia, Kouch, Lunda, Lower Kongo, Ngola and Luba.

● Despite the approbation given by some emperors to the slave trade, the formation of these large empires helped to arrest the depopulation.

● Ethiopia was incessantly plundered and disorganized by the powers of the Middle East, and in turn organized punitive expeditions into Arabia and Yemen.

● This hardly stopped the villainous behaviour of the trading companies established by the great merchant bourgeoisies of Cairo, Basra, Shiraz and Marrakesh. Indeed, from AD 632 onwards, they used the propagation of Islam as a pretext to plunder the countries they conquered.

The Middle Ages

All the societies in north and north-west Africa were thrown into disorder in the ninth century by the attacks of the Almoravides. The fall of the empire of Ghana was due to their pressure. Millions were obliged to emigrate from north-west Africa (Mauretania, Senegal, Mali) to the coastal regions where the severity of the climate is well known. A similar exodus took place from northern and eastern Africa.

The wilful destruction which accompanied this search for riches was the source of many movements of the population and was responsible for the appearance of new trading centres controlled by the African rulers and the merchants of the Middle East.

A number of towns became important relays in the slave trade, organized by the metropolises of the Middle East and the large Mediterranean cities. Among these towns we can count Zanzibar, Pemba, Kilwa, Mombasa, Quelimane, Mogadiscio, Benin, Gondar, Timbuktu, Marrakesh, Moroni, Kairouan, Dar-es-Salaam and Khartoum. For almost 1,000 years, the merchants of the Middle East and their African associates levied a toll of slaves on the African peoples who, despite a dogged and increasing resistance, were obliged to seek refuge elsewhere and so ceaselessly to move hither and thither.

Europe Expands its Influence

After five centuries of Moorish domination, Spain and Portugal took over the African slave trade from the Moors. They furnished manpower to their colonies in the Americas and the Caribbean thanks to this revolting commerce. The galleons of the Iberian peninsula ran up and down the African coasts, seeking new riches — spices, gold and ivory — but above all seeking slaves, to work in the agricultural industries (sugar cane, coffee, cocoa, spices) of the conquered territories, which had been stripped of their native populations. This tragic adventure continued for over five centuries. Historians estimate that it cost the continent of Africa 100 million inhabitants.

It began in 1415, when the ruling classes of Portugal organized military expeditions into the African hinterland, occupying the towns of Ceuta, Madeira, Rio de Oro and Tangier, and inflicting a brutal war on the kingdom of Morocco. With the help of certain African kinglets, who owed their power to economic and social decadence, the Portuguese merchants established new trading posts by the power of the sword or the gun: among others in Sierra Leone (1474), at Cape Verde, in the Benin (now Dahomey and Nigeria), Sâo Tomé and Principe, at Sâo Jorge de Mina (now Ghana) in 1482, at Santa Maria d'Angola, Sofala, Quelimane, Mombasa, Mogadiscio, Diego-Suarez, Gondar and the Mascareignes (now Reunion and Mauritius).

The kingdom of Portugal embarked on a colonial adventure built on slavery, of which the leaders were to be Vasco da Gama, Diego Diaz, Bartholomeu Diaz, Francisco de Almeida, Diego Cam and Fernaô Gomez.

Wherever these men led their ships of war, their looting left devastation and desolation. The peoples they met were forced to choose between giving in to their demands for slaves or beating back into the forests behind the coasts.

Later, other European states such as the Netherlands, Great Britain and France were to follow the example of Portugal and take far more ruthless initiatives.

The inhuman commerce of African slaves, sold in the Americas by these countries, was to allow the accumulation of capital which launched the industrialization of Europe and North America in the 18th Century.

Such are the beginnings of the imperialist period of the capitalist states, for the same governments were to continue with the direct colonization of Africa, considered as a dumping ground for the manufactured products of the growing industries.

Already drained of their populations by the slave trade, the African peoples were subjected to colonial wars for a century. Ill prepared for modern warfare, most of them were obliged to flee or perish. The Herero people in Namibia are a good example of this. Formerly they possessed enormous pastoral wealth, but in the 19th Century the Germans under Bismarck robbed and exterminated them. All over the continent, peoples were transported from one region to another at the mercy of every natural hazard: disease, malnutrition, famine, for example. The huge colonial companies held them at their beck and call: that was how France produced peanut-oil in Senegal, how Belgium got rubber, metal (copper and cobalt) and diamonds from the Congo, and how in the Gold Coast (now Ghana) Great Britain exploited gold and cocoa.

New towns were built everywhere, inhabited mainly by the refugees chased off their lands by the colonial wars. Examples are Saint Louis in Senegal, Brazzaville, Libreville, Pointe Noire, Tema, Windhoek and Capetown. Whole tribal societies were destroyed, while others emerged, constituted by the assemblage of several tribes. And all this was to be confirmed by the division of Africa agreed to in 1885 by the colonial powers.

The colonial system imposed forced labour to build the large structures (dams, roads, railways) which were to allow easier penetration and give greater access to the continent. Naturally this increased the number of refugees.

Compulsory incorporation of Africans in the colonial armies obliged all the young men who were fit for service to flee or to go into exile in their thousands. Under Clémenceau 400,000 foot soldiers were conscripted by France during the war of 1914–18, and Great Britain acted in the same way.

Nationalist or religious revolts led the colonial powers to transplant whole populations. We can quote as examples the Mahdists in Anglo-Egyptian Sudan, the Moslem sects known as the Tidianists and the Hamalists in French Sudan (now Mali) and in Senegal, and the Kibanguists, who represent a syncretism of African, Moslem and Catholic values, in the Congo. All these religions and their followers have been persecuted by the colonial powers and have swelled the ranks of the refugees.

The part played by the Africans in the war of 1939–45 to free Europe from the yoke of nazism was more or less the determining factor which made them conscious of their right to determine their future. Nationalist movements began to arise and combat colonialism on the political field.

From 1957 on, the African territories were granted independence. We might be tempted to think that the wave of refugees would come to an end.

But new events, alas, were to swell the already lengthy procession of refugees in the continent. A new process of indirect colonization appeared, which increased the economic and ideological grip of the colonial powers in an overwhelming manner, while allowing them the appearance of new political rights. The colonial powers left their colonies by the back door, only to come in again by the front.

This hypocritical way of acting aroused the feeling among some nationalists that colonial domination should be rejected once and for all.

On the other hand, certain powers, like Spain and Portugal, refused to grant independence.

Wars for national freedom broke out everywhere. In Algeria in 1954, and at the same period in the Cameroons. Guinea-Bissau, Angola, Mozambique, Zimbabwe, Namibia, South Africa and the Western Sahara followed in the 1960s, 1970s and 1980s, each new outburst again bringing in its wake thousands of refugees.

In the meantime, the economic consequences of the discovery of diamond mines created new confrontations between local populations and the colonial powers. Numerous coups d'état took place, at the instigation or with the support of neo-colonial metropolises jealous of their privileges; again the consequences were hordes of political refugees and stateless persons, and countless massacres and assassinations. Even sporting events became the arena of covert political manoeuvres, and caused huge movements of the population and massive expulsions. Such were also the effect of wars and putsches carried out by mercenaries hired by former colonial powers.

Since 'Independence'

But colonial capitalism had no intention of relinquishing its political and military interests. After a short period in which it played the game of political capitulation and granted a purely nominal independence, it again set loose on the continent conflicts which had their origin apparently in ethnic and religious differences or in sporting rivalry. But these civil wars, intensified by natural catastrophes, famines and the inveterate shortage of food supplies, have been regularly fostered by the transnational corporations (TNCs).

The following list will give an idea of some of these events which have produced, throughout the continent, important movements of refugees:

1) In 1956, the British army in Sierra Leone expelled from their holdings numbers of Africans searching for diamonds. They were parked in camps or expelled in their thousands, at the instigation of the colonial diamond companies.

2) In 1957, in the north-west of the continent, in the Ivory Coast, Africans had been exploiting diamond-bearing concessions for many years. They were chased out by the thousand and sent back to their native territories. Today, as a consequence of twenty years' unrestrained exploitation by a French company with little or no interest in the Ivory Coast, these mines have been shut down.

3) In 1958, just before independence was granted to the Ivory Coast, there was a massive expulsion, by the French colonial army, of Dahomans and Togolais living in this territory. No serious explanation was given, but the main reason seems to have been that these men and women were progressive contractors, business men and civil servants: their presence would have been an obstacle to the neo-colonial plans which had been drawn up for the period following the granting of independence.

4) In 1958 Guinea-Conakry became unilaterally independent under the control of the Democratic Party of Guinea (PDG). The result of the anti-nationalist propaganda launched by the French government of de Gaulle at the time was to incite more than a million of them to choose exile in the neighbouring countries (mainly in Senegal and the Ivory Coast) both before and after these became independent in 1960.

5) In 1960 a revolt broke out in South Sudan against the military regime of Khartoum. It was supported first and foremost by the Emperor of Ethiopia, Haile Selassie, and by some groups in the Roman Catholic Church. This revolt became a religious conflict between the Moslems of the north and the Christians of the south. Thousands of Sudanese took refuge in Ethiopia, under the leadership of charitable organizations, often of a confessional nature.

6) From 1960 to 1965 the Belgian Congo (by now known as Zaire) became a battlefield. NATO employed its ideological and military strength to oppose the Congolese patriots who sought true national sovereignty for their country, including the control of its natural resources. All the leaders of the nationalist cause were slaughtered (Lumumba), and the people put to the sword.

To what solutions could the people turn in their distress? They could only flee and take shelter wherever possible. NATO and the Atlantic Alliance succeeded finally in putting at the helm a team which is still on their side.

The evil done is still going on.

7) The discovery of oil in the region of Nigeria known as Biafra aroused rivalry between transnational corporations, each of which was backed by

a capitalist government. Thus the French government was behind the demands of the people of Biafra for secession, whereas the central government of Nigeria was supported by Great Britain and the United States.

8) In 1975 a terrible drought struck the Sahel (the zone bordering the south of the Sahara). Thousands of people sought refuge in regions where the climate was more temperate.

9) The UN decided that the populations of the Western Sahara had the right of self-determination, but Morocco attempted to increase the size of its national territory. War thus broke out between the kingdom of Morocco and the nationalists of the Polisario Front. At present there are nearly 50,000 Sahraoui refugees in Algeria and in other parts of the Sahara.

10) In 1977 a war broke out between Somalia and Ethiopia. The rulers of these two countries have been at loggerheads for many centuries over the claims of each side to possess the Ogaden, presently a region of Ethiopia. Three million Somalis living in the Ogaden took refuge in Somalia and at Djibouti. At the same time the nationalist and military government of Ethiopia failed to find a basis of agreement with the liberation fronts of Eritrea and the province of Tigre. The war between them increased in violence and thousands of Eritreans were obliged to take refuge in Sudan, at Djibouti and in the Arab countries along the Persian Gulf.

These wars are still going on.

11) In 1978 some Zairese refugees, who had taken up arms and organized themselves as a national front, occupied the large mining area of the Shaba with the complicity of the inhabitants. The forces of the Atlantic Alliance attacked and the nationalists withdrew. They tried again, but the armed forces of the Alliance remained in the Shaba to protect the copper mines.

As a result, thousands of refugees left the country for Zambia.

12) In 1983 two million workers from Ghana, Chad and other countries, were expelled from Nigeria on economic pretexts and sent back to their own countries.

13) Chad, which has always been a restless area, is again the centre of a war, the different factions in the country being supported by foreign powers with opposing interests. Libya takes the part of the Transitional Government of National Union (GUNT) of Goukouni Oueddei, while the United States threatens the French leadership in the region and compels France to send troops in support of the government of Hissen Habré ('Operation MANTA'). In 1984 the simultaneous withdrawal of French and Libyan troops (despite some recoils on the part of the Libyans) has left the northern front quiet. Not so, however, in the south, where there are new outbreaks of violence.

14) Today there are still thousands of refugees on the run from the racist mercenary forces fighting in the wars of Namibia, Angola, Mozambique and South Africa. A million Blacks have been expelled from the so-called

White zones of the RSA, and sent to areas which are unknown to them. In March 1984, the RSA began to reap the fruits of its policy of terror and ruin. By supporting the National Union for the Total Independence of Angola (UNITA) and the National Resistance of Mozambique (MNR), the RSA has unsettled and economically exhausted Angola and Mozambique. These two great countries of the Front Line are at the end of their tether and obliged to come to terms. The aim of the RSA is to ensure that the Cubans leave Angola, to prepare a neo-colonial 'independence' for Namibia, and to suppress the rearguard bases used by the South West African People's Organization (SWAPO) and the African National Congress (ANC).

As the wheel of history never stops turning, there will be no end to the flow of refugees as long as the pillage of Africa's resources continues, and as long as it is made possible by the lack of unity among the popular forces of the continent and the absence of democracy.

2. The French Colonial Heritage

People and groups obliged to leave their country to assure their livelihood are 'refugees' in the strict sense of this term. It is interesting to remember that large numbers of refugees and huge exoduses were already well known in Black Africa long before the days of 'independence'. They are part of colonial history. And that throws light on what is happening today even if, as we have shown in the preceding chapter, the same phenomena were to be observed among the populations south of the Sahara prior to the colonial period.

Colonization and the systems it introduced led people to leave their homes, as we have already said, to avoid compulsory conscription in the army or in the hordes of workers recruited for public works projects. In many cases, the artificial nature of the colonial frontiers, which often divided homogeneous ethnic groups, made the flight of the refugees easier.

This is what we are going to explain with the help of some significant examples taken from former French colonies. None of them was in the zones studied at the meeting of 6 November, but it would be incorrect to believe that they have been spared or that there are no movements of population in them even today.

Escaping Conscription and Forced Labour

In 1923, Albert Sarraut (then Minister for the Colonies) published his book, *The Development of the French Colonies* (Editions Payot). He gave the number of infantry who were enrolled from 1914 to 1918: a total of 193,349 for French West Africa and 17,910 for French Equatorial Africa, in all 211,259 men for the French colonies in Black Africa.

To avoid conscription, which was becoming more and more compulsory, and its methods, the populations of West Africa, and especially of French Sudan (now Mali) and Upper Volta, sought refuge in the Gold Coast (now Ghana), in Togo, in Sierra Leone and in Liberia. Others attempted to resist, and revolts were put down with bloodshed as early as 1915 among the Bambara, and then in the region of the Volta, among the Tuaregs, in the Atakora and even in the Ivory Coast.

19

We find the same sequence, obligatory recruitment followed by bloody repression, in Equatorial Africa, from the Cameroons to Middle Congo. In 1917 the infamous massacre of Abeche took place, described by General Hilary, in his book *From the Congo to the Nile* (published in Marseilles in 1930), as: 'an atrocious tragedy, exceeding in cruelty and horror even the most bloody extravagances of the former sultans, which threw the whole country into a panic and left for a long period a terror-stricken souvenir' (p. 328). Here the refugees were running away as much from the repression as from the recruitment.

The victory of the Allies was to foster the development of another factor of depopulation, already present during the war: the flight to escape from forced labour. The compulsory growing of cotton in Upper Volta is worth quoting, as Governor-General Robert Delavignette has attempted to give the figures in his book *The True Chiefs of the Empire* (published by Gallimard, Paris, in 1927 and 1929). He estimates that before the Second World War this obligation had already persuaded 100,000 Mossi to flee to the Gold Coast alone. Another example is better known and has been popularized in two books by André Gide: *Journey to Congo* and *Return from Chad* (published by Gallimard, 1927 and 1928). He tells of the construction of the railway from Brazzaville to Pointe Noire, between 1921 and 1934, which employed thousands of workers. They were first of all levied in the Congo itself, and later brought in from Gabon, Ubangi-Shari (now the Central African Republic) and Chad. Governor-General Antonetti, who made this construction his life's work, is said to have declared: 'I need ten thousand dead for my railway.'[1] Indeed, Albert Londres confirms that the death toll of the workers on this construction exceeded 30% between 1927 and 1929.[2] The result was a series of revolts and repressions throughout French Equatorial Africa right up to 1930, but also the desperate flight of thousands of people, as a result of which Ubangi-Shari lost a third of its population.[3]

Artificial Frontiers

Run away from army recruitment and from forced labour, flee the repressions which followed the revolts, and other disasters as well, but where were people to go?

At the time, French colonies in Africa were administered in the framework of the federations of French West Africa and French Equatorial Africa, each of which had held a territory under mandate since the Treaty of Versailles. The real refuge, or at least the safest, was to cross the borders of French colonialism, for within them the chase given to fugitives and the repression they suffered generally escaped the condemnations of the international authorities. And if the refugees found on the other side of these borders peoples with languages and customs similar to theirs, many difficulties were overcome.

If we want to understand better the artificial nature of these frontiers, we must bear in mind the vast migrations and movements of population to which most of the Black populations were accustomed prior to colonization. These had often come to an end with the colonial period, which brought to a close the rivalries between clans and kingdoms, and even the wider conflicts between larger socio-religious masses in which the losers had to give way to the winners or accept their domination.

The divisions of the African continent into different zones of European influence took place among peoples in constant migration: this made the frontiers drawn over them even more artificial. This is not only the case for the countries in the eastern zone of the Sahel. There is nothing strange in the fact that the frontiers of Ghana, Nigeria and the Belgian Congo cut across peoples speaking the same language or parent languages. The agreements reached by the British, the French and the Germans took very little account of this. And so we can consider that a Ewe from French Dahomey or Togo felt less 'foreign' among his fellow tribesmen in British Togo or in Ghana than he would have felt had he been transported into the mountains of the Banfora. In French West Africa, the peoples of the forest are often divided into tribes whose territories cross the continent horizontally, whereas the colonies possessed frontiers disposed vertically with respect to the shore. This fact is too well known for us to insist on it here.

On the other hand, this same artificiality of the federal and colonial frontiers can throw a new light on the concept of a 'refugee' before the granting of 'independence'. Peoples could be forcibly displaced from their ethnic territories while remaining within the boundaries of the same colony. African history between 1920 and 1960 is full of examples of such displacements, which are in large part responsible for the settlement in towns and suburbs of people from lands which have been conceded to the colonial companies. They flock to the towns in a refugee situation and with a refugee mentality.

The permanence and even the development of people's ethnic consciousness can be remarked in certain countries of French-speaking Black Africa even today, when a national consciousness is beginning to unite peoples living within the borders inherited from the colonial era. It is a powerful cause of economic and political solidarities which, despite the inequalities developed by capitalism among the members of a tribe, allow those who are less favoured to survive their misfortune, or at least to hope that survival is possible . . . according to whether the tribe they belong to is a 'winner' or a 'loser'.

In most cases, to displace people far from their tribal territory, even within the limits of a same 'nation', will leave them not only with a refugee mentality, but also with the economic, political and cultural situation we find among all refugees.

Notes

1. Sources quoted by Jean Suret-Canale in *Black Africa — The Colonial Era*, vol. 2 (Paris, Éditions Sociales), p. 264. (1st edition 1964; 2nd edition 1977.)
2. Ibid.
3. Cf. P. Kalck, *Histoire de la République Centrafricaine* (Paris, Berger-Levrault, 1974).

3. Recent Facts and Figures

In 1983, the number of African refugees, if we use this term in its widest sense, was estimated at 6 million. Of these, some 2,672,500 were refugees in the narrower sense used by the Geneva Convention in 1952, but there were also some 3,366,300 persons displaced within their own country by climatic conditions, by wars and by unfavourable economic policies, and this is why the meaning of the term should be revised and enlarged. The number of people in both groups has increased since then and is indeed growing every day.

One out of every three refugees is from Africa. The principal reasons for this are as follows:

● The effects of colonialism: the frontier was drawn arbitrarily when independence was granted, separating people with the same culture among several countries. African politicians have exploited this situation.

● The violation in Africa of human rights: several dictatorial regimes have come to power since the 1960s in Africa, and some have disappeared. This has resulted in massacres, torture, expropriation, arbitrary imprisonment, tribal and religious discrimination, war between the countries. And all this led the people to flee in huge numbers.

● Economic inequality between the different countries: certain 'blocks' which are well developed have attracted more and more people, without necessarily finding work for them.

● Natural calamities (such as floods and droughts) have often made the plight of the refugees worse.

● The victims of apartheid in South Africa and Namibia have fled to the neighbouring countries.

Where do they come from?

More than 90% of the refugees come from below the Sahara and live in this part of the continent. Among the most shocking cases we can cite:

Angola: 232,000 Angolans are still in Zaire, waiting to go home. It is estimated that 50,000 return each year.

Ethiopia: This country holds the sad record in Africa for the number of refugees. There were some 1,743,800 in 1983 (by the strict definition), to which should be added 2,400,000 persons displaced within the country because of the wars (Eritrea, Ogaden, Sidamo and Tigré), the permanent violations of human rights and natural calamities. Look at Table 3.2 and you will see that one refugee out of two is Ethiopian. Some 150,000 Ethiopians were reported to have returned from neighbouring countries, but it remains difficult to achieve any certainty as to the real numbers.

Uganda: There were 185,000 refugees from this country in 1983, of whom 150,000 had fled to Zaire after the troubles which led to the fall of Amin Dada. At the end of 1983, the government claimed that 300,000 of the 485,000 refugees who had fled at this time were back in the country. But as the return was spontaneous and unorganized, no serious reliance on these figures is possible.

The *Namibians* and the *South Africans* either go to neighbouring countries (Angola, Swaziland, Lesotho) or to countries which belong to the 'Front' which actively supports the movements of national liberation (Tanzania and Zambia).

The refugees in *Africa north of the Sahara* are principally in Algeria, where there are 150,000 Sahraouis. Egypt has also accepted some 5,500 refugees, most of whom are from East Africa.

Table 3.1
The Number of Refugees in the World (July 1982) and the Regions which Host Them

Africa	2,672,500
Asia and the Middle East	4,977,700[a]
Latin America	299,200
North America and Europe	2,262,700[b]
Total	*10,212,100*
Total in other countries	*100,000[c]*
Grand Total	*10,312,100*

[a] 1,000,000 of these are in Iran, and most of them come from Afghanistan.
[b] The United States hosts 1,003,500, Canada has received 353,000 and France 150,000.
[c] This total includes all countries which have received fewer than 500 each. The figures in this list come from the list published by the High Commission for Refugees (Geneva).

The Burden of Hosting Them

As for the countries which receive them, the most tragic concentration of refugees is in East Africa, and the main cause is the problem of Ethiopia.

Somalia: A Somali source says that the country has received 1,300,000 Ethiopian refugees. This constitutes 36% of the total population. It is easy to understand the economic, political and social difficulties that result for this country, which is one of the poorest in Africa and which, in turn, is a regular victim of drought and floods.

Djibouti: In 1982, 42,000 Ethiopian refugees (13% of the total population of Djibouti) were registered. In 1984, the estimates speak of 25,000. Despite the drop in numbers, the young republic, which has only been independent for four years, is suffering from serious economic difficulties. There is no agriculture and no industry, and the main revenues are derived from port charges and French subsidies. To that must be added the tribal problems rooted in the traditional rivalry between the Afars and the Issa.

Sudan: This country has very limited resources. In the middle of 1983, the government counted 665,000 refugees, of whom 460,000 were from Ethiopia, 200,000 from Uganda and 5,000 from Zaire.

Table 3.2
Provenance and Numbers of Refugees and Displaced Persons (April 1981)

Country	Refugees	Displaced persons
Angola	232,000	50,000
Burundi	149,200	100,000
Ethiopia	1,743,800	2,400,000
Uganda	185,500	335,000
Central African Republic	15,000	—
Cameroons	—	35,000
Rwanda	101,000	36,300
Sudan	11,000	60,000
Chad	352,540	—
Zaire	63,000	—
Zambia	20,000	—
Zimbabwe	—	250,000
Equatorial Guinea	23,000	—
Namibia	52,500	—
Republic of South Africa	35,600	—
Total	*2,966,100*	*3,366,300*

(The figures in Table 3.2 are taken from the national reports presented at the International Conference on Assistance to Refugees in Africa — (ICARA I) held on 9–10 April 1981. The difference between 'refugees' and 'displaced persons' will be explained below (Chapter 13).)

Table 3.3
Estimate of the Number of Refugees in Africa and Changes over a
Fifteen-Month Period

Host country	Number in April '81	Number in July '82	Difference
Algeria	—	167,000	—
Angola	73,000	93,600	+20,600
Botswana	1,000	1,300	+300
Burundi	200,000	214,000	+14,000
Congo	10,000	—	—
Djibouti	42,000	31,600	−10,400
Egypt	—	5,500	—
Ethiopia	11,000	11,000	Nil
Ghana	250	—	—
Kenya	3,500	4,000	+500
Lesotho	10,000	11,500	+1,500
Liberia	200	—	—
Morocco	—	500	—
Nigeria	105,000	100,000	−5,000
Uganda	113,000	113,000	Nil
Central African Republic	6,540	4,000	−2,540
Cameroons	266,000	3,400	−262,600[a]
Tanzania	150,000	174,000	+24,000
Rwanda	10,150	18,000	+7,850
Senegal	5,000	4,000	−1,000
Sierra Leone	400	—	—
Somalia	1,300,000	700,000	−600,000[b]
Sudan	438,000	627,000	+189,000
Swaziland	6,000	5,800	−200
Zaire	400,000	325,000	−75,000[c]
Zambia	36,000	58,300	+22,300
Total	*3,187,040*	*2,672,500*	*−514,540*

[a]The strong fall in the number of refugees in the Cameroons between these two dates can be attributed to a massive return of people from Chad.

[b]The first figure is that given by the Somali government, asking for assistance in its report to ICARA I. The second that of the High Commission for Refugees in the official basis for a plan of assistance. On the other hand, we know that the war is far from finished, even if less violent, so we cannot reasonably conclude that 600,000 people have gone home! How carefully we must study the figures presented!

[c]According to the Angolan government report for ICARA I, some 50,000 Angolan refugees return home every year.

Conclusion

The assistance and administration of refugees and displaced persons is a burden too heavy for Africa, over-exploited and ravaged by wars and internal divisions as she is. So she looks again with hope to the international community.

As a consequence of the International Conference on Assistance to Refugees in Africa (ICARA I) held on 9–10 April 1981, a certain number of states agreed to give a total of US$570,000,000 to help. According to the report sent by the Secretariat of the High Commission for Refugees to the Executive Committee established to manage these funds, they were to be used to 'stabilize the situation, tide over the crises and find lasting solutions'. But ICARA I has failed to achieve its primary aim, which was to mobilize the necessary resources to allow the host countries to finance the economic, administrative and social infrastructures necessary to face up to the extra burden which the arrival of refugees constitutes for countries without resources.

That is why the General Assembly of the UN decided, on 18 December 1982, to hold a second International Conference on Assistance to Refugees in Africa (ICARA II). The principal objectives of this conference were to be:

● to evaluate ICARA I and see how far the projects it decided on had been put into effect;

● to study in what degree those who are strictly speaking 'refugees' and those who have returned to their country need further help;

● to circumscribe and evaluate the burden imposed on the countries which host refugees by the strengthening of their economic and social infrastructures.

This conference took place at Geneva from 9–11 July 1984 (see below, Chapter 15).

Part 2:
General Causes
and Responsibilities

4. American Policy in Africa

The policy of the United States in Africa reflects the aims of the Cold War and the struggle to gain influence against the forward thrust of the countries of the Communist bloc, especially the USSR, Cuba and East Germany.

After the Second World War the United States noted uneasily that the colonial powers, victorious but economically weakened, were unable to allow their former colonies or protectorates a sufficiently liberal economic growth to allow the popular masses of Africa to recover from their poverty. For the Americans this poverty, and the contrasting luxury of the settlers, was grist to the mill of communist ideology and strengthened the influence of the Eastern countries under the leadership of the USSR. That is why the USA furnished clandestine assistance to the anti-colonial movements and why the CIA watched over the Black intelligentsia which was developing in the universities. This was a political strategy, but it also served their economic interests in the long run, even equipping them to rival Europe.

The Reagan administration has reinforced the strategy of blocs, negating the overtures made by the Carter government, especially by Andrew Young, American representative at the UN.

In recent times, however, Washington appears to wish to revise the oversimplistic reactionary positions which were so vigorously affirmed in 1980. This is probably due to pressure from businessmen, to analyses made by the information services and to the influence of George Schultz, who has replaced General Haig at the head of the State Department.

So we have to describe a policy that is not undifferentiated, but one that is in flux and often contradicts itself. It is in flux, because each region has its own specific characteristics, and the USA now seems to want to take them into account. It is contradictory for the very same reason. On the one hand, Washington tries to support unstable regimes in order to create a certain political stability on the continent, because changes in the system of power are frequently favourable to Soviet-Cuban influences. On the other hand, America's open support of friendly regimes, notably that of South Africa, has the effect of reinforcing the positions of the Front Line countries which it alienates even more from any eventual co-operation with the USA.

This policy is also contradictory because the interests at stake are not coherent. The business world proclaims more and more clearly the difference between the economic and the political interests, and this does not make the American tactics any clearer.

This is the background against which we must see the recent diversity of American proposals of assistance, the new diplomatic openings towards countries regarded as 'progressive', and the effort to adapt American positions. Such was the recent visit of Chester Crocker to Mozambique, after months of diplomatic and economic warfare; such also the openings made in the direction of the progressive countries of the Indian Ocean at the initiative of Schultz, who is considered as the representative of the pragmatic, down-to-earth business world.

American Policy in the Different Regions

Southern Africa

Until recently the position of the Reagan administration could be summarized in the following points:
— Reinforce the support given by the USA to the Republic of South Africa (RSA);
— Freeze relations with Mozambique and take a punitive attitude towards Angola, clearly with the goal of changing the famous Clark Amendment which, since 1976, has forbidden any form of American aid to Savimbi (UNITA);
— Maintain that there must be correlation between the acceptance of a settlement in Namibia and a retreat of Cuban forces from Angola which could lead to Savimbi's participation in the Angolan government.

There was no doubt who was meant when Washington spoke about 'the friendly country'. Chester Crocker, responsible for African affairs in the State Department, affirmed: 'The US must say clearly that they have no intention of getting involved on the slippery ground of economic sanctions towards the RSA.' Richard Allen, director of the National Security Council and co-ordinator of American foreign policy, stated that American action in southern Africa must be based on the exclusive interests of America in the RSA. And Caspar Weinberger, responsible for Defense, declared that the RSA must become 'the muscular guardian' of the region before this role was assumed by the USSR or by Cuba.

Outpost of western interests, guardian of the free world, the South African regime also produces large quantities of strategic ores. According to certain American specialists, if the supply were to be interrupted, the US would need five or ten years to recover from the shock! This is a matter for reflection — if we need one.

The two states share numerous objectives, among which we can count the dislocation of the revolutionary process underway in Angola and Mozambique, which they both see as an obstacle to the defence of their interests in the region. We shall see that this analysis is severely called into question on the other side of the Atlantic.

So the Reagan administration has strengthened the alliance between the two countries and taken numerous decisions in favour of the RSA, both in the economic and the political fields. To give an example, the Department of Commerce has proposed extending the limits placed on exports when these affect products to be used by the military or police forces of the RSA.

This radicalization of American policy has of course harmed Mozambique, which has suffered from the cessation of food aid since the expulsion of American diplomats accused of working for the CIA. Angola and Mozambique are thus subjected to the stranglehold of economic and military threats and subversive operations conducted within their frontiers by both Pretoria and Washington.

This picture was a faithful application of the Reagan doctrine until the last months of 1982, but it seems that it needs correcting as from this date. Changes have been made which seem to suggest that Washington has adopted a new point of view and is applying a more responsive policy.

Is the American government becoming aware of the confusion in which its policy leaves the question of Namibia? It declares openly that 'any possible settlement in Namibia must pass by America', but it is becoming clear that this problem is a major obstacle to their policy in Africa. Several attitudes are possible here:

1) Washington can decide to support the RSA unconditionally: to use the right of veto on every possible occasion, and to approve and give financial and military support to the struggle against SWAPO. But if America does this she will be totally isolated in Africa. At least 50 states have affirmed this at the UN, of whom Nigeria is an important partner for the Americans. At the same time they have let other western states (notably France) overtake them, because these states have adopted a much more flexible position on the question.

2) Washington remains satisfied with an attitude of conciliation, which leaves the RSA free to continue her policy of aggression.

3) The American government will come to realize that its advantage lies in finding a real solution to the Namibian problem, and will in consequence adopt a more positive attitude towards SWAPO and its allies. In so doing, the US will offset the influence of the USSR and improve its own position in the region.

'Secret' negotiations are now going on, in the hope of bringing Pretoria to accept the latest western proposals on the subject, which represent a compromise between the desires of the different parties to the dispute.

It is of course impossible to count with certainty on any one outcome to these negotiations. But a change can be seen in the American attitude, notably with regard to Mozambique, where Chester Crocker went on 13

January 1983, followed by the Agency for International Development (AID), which is often a cover used for missions to form African police forces. This latter agency came to study how to resume and increase food aid, and to investigate the possibility of economic assistance.

On the other hand, the increase in South African aggression, in order to make a settlement of the Namibian question impossible, is a confirmation of the fact that the American position has evolved.

As the Americans themselves declare, the US has indeed a determining part to play in bringing equilibrium to southern Africa or giving it over to destruction. The choice will probably be simply the result of the comparison between the advantages and disadvantages, political, economic and diplomatic, in each hypothesis. The stakes of the game are of considerable value, as they are no less than the military, economic and political state of a whole region and the peoples living in it.

The Horn of Africa
Here again, the Cold War is in full swing, making use of other countries and the bodies of other peoples.

The problem is simple: Ethiopia has an important geo-strategic position, close to the Arab peninsula and the route used by the oil tankers. It forms an excellent base for the penetration of Africa, and its present government is upheld by the USSR and South Yemen. In June 1977 its neighbour, Somalia, which in 1974 had signed a treaty of friendship with Moscow, invaded the Ethiopian province of the Ogaden. When Moscow upheld Ethiopia, Somalia broke off her diplomatic relations with the USSR. The US remained neutral, fearing to compromise its position in Africa by helping an aggressor and hoping that Ethiopia would turn out to be a hornets' nest for the Eastern countries.

But the intervention of the Soviets in Afghanistan changed the situation. The Americans consider that the presence of the Red Army in the warm seas is a danger and that they are much too close to the oil which is to be found in the Gulf. The Soviets have already set up a base at Berbera, which is at the entry to the Red Sea and only 120 miles from the Ethiopian border.

The American government has bases at Masirak (in Oman) and Mombasa (Kenya) and enjoys the support of Egypt and Sudan in the region. On 24 August 1980, Washington completed its panoply of defence against Soviet 'imperialism' by signing an agreement with Mogadiscio for military and economic co-operation. In return for the possibilities thus offered to him, Reagan declared on 21 October 1982, the thirteenth anniversary of the Somali revolution: 'I promise you our support and our active help in your defence against the unjust aggression of which your country is the victim . . .' How words can change their meaning according to the circumstances.

Indeed, from 1980 to 1985, Somalia, Sudan and Kenya have received almost 50% of American military aid in Africa. And beyond this military support, these countries have the advantage of help from the Security Support Fund Programme, designed to assure the economic and political stability of states believed to be weak. And in the Horn of Africa is to be found the base of the Rapid Deployment Force, renamed in 1983 the US Central Command (USCENTCOM). This force has been completely reshuffled by Reagan, who has an enormously heavy offensive machine which bears no resemblance to the light intervention force provided for by Carter. We should probably see behind this the pressure exerted by the military-industrial complex and the huge increase in military expenditure decided by the administration of Reagan. But here again, the attitude of America does not seem to be definitely fixed.

Indeed Washington still believes that Ethiopia could return to the western camp. Colonel Mengistu's regime is more clearly marked by its nationalism than by an unconditional attachment to Moscow. Many high officials in Ethiopia consider this simply as the consequence of the country's need for armaments and for logistic and economic support.

The Indian Ocean

This zone provides us with a good example of the change in the attitude of Reagan's administration.

Faced with economic crisis, ideological sympathies give way to financial necessities, and only the western countries and their institutions can provide the solution. Seeing that the USSR is losing the race in the area, the American government seized a chance to enlarge its influence and embarked on a huge operation of seduction, spending dollars profusely, of course. The undertaking is directed towards several states in the area which were formerly considered as progressive.

In *Madagascar*, the US opened an embassy, increased food aid, and sent in the CIA to 'control the success' of the election of Ratsiraka.

In *Mauritius*, the MMM Party was attacked and undermined by Washington before it came to power, but its leaders Paul Bérenger and Jean-Claude de l'Estrac were warmly received by the American government, which gave its unreserved support to the demands they made on the International Monetary Fund and the World Bank. But after nine months' uncertainty and immobility, the people of Mauritius were again called to vote. The elections put in power Jugnauth and Duval in a right-wing coalition. And as the foreign debt is more than 700 million dollars, the island has become a hostage to the IMF, and in this way is obliged to follow American policy.

In *the Seychelles*, the US named an ambassador for the first time. The man chosen was David Joseph Fisher, a specialist in east-west relations. Chester Crocker declared recently, while speaking about the Seychelles: 'We take this country seriously, as we have important interests there' (we can perceive the usual American undertones!) '. . . we mean to do everything we can to get the advantages we need.' They have already partially obtained these advantages, as Washington possesses in the country an important station to locate satellites, which employs 200 technicians and brings the country an annual income of 2 million dollars, to which should be added the 1.3 million dollars spent on construction.

The Letter of the Indian Ocean bore the headline, on 24 December 1982: 'The Indian Ocean becomes an American Lake?' Indeed America already has 230,000 men of the Rapid Intervention Force on the spot, as well as an aircraft-carrier with a capacity of 100 planes. It is continuing to move its pawns to strategic positions (such as Chagos) for the defence of the oil routes and the affirmation of its opposition to the Soviet Union.

To realize this policy, the US is now turning towards countries which are progressive but belong to the movement of non-aligned states, following the policy advocated by François Mitterrand, who has said that even if we do not share the point of view of certain countries, it is better to give them all the help they desire than to allow them to fall prey to Soviet influence. And indeed M. Mitterrand only expressed the arguments of many African politicians for whom, the goal being economic development, it matters little in the last resort which power provides the help they need.

American Economic Policy in Africa

Economics is closely linked to politics. In certain cases, the American business world will disagree with the analyses and the interests supported by the government and will try to influence the positions taken by politicians. Angola is a case in point. Elsewhere, for example in the attitude towards the RSA, government policy will influence the investments and the commercial position of American firms. And then the economic analyses of the information agencies can result in abrupt changes of commercial policy, creating disastrous results in the economies of countries which suffer the consequences (as in Nigeria).

The two characteristics of the American economic position in Africa are its extreme overall weakness and its unequal distribution throughout the continent. Africa below the Sahara is greatly privileged.

In the last twenty years, investments in Africa, generally in the mining and oil extracting sectors, have represented only 3% of American investments in the world. The cause of this weakness is largely historical: the links between the two continents are very recent. But they are also political: Africa has only recently been recognized as an important zone by the American administration, and they are also economic: as American firms find it difficult to adapt to perpetually changing socio-political situations, and the African states take back control of their economic resources. The privileged place of Africa below the Sahara is illustrated by the high concentration of American investments in Liberia (rubber), in Ghana and Zambia (mines), in Zaire, but above all in the RSA and Nigeria.

Trade relations, largely complementary to the policy of investments, and protecting access to certain markets, have more or less the same characteristics. Sub-Saharan Africa, destined to play a major role in what Haig called the 'war of resources', represents 60% of the trade between America and Africa; 70% of the trade with Africa south of the Sahara is with the RSA and Nigeria.

The heavy dependence of the US on five African minerals should be noted. American dependency for supplies of cobalt, chrome, manganese, platinum and industrial diamonds is everywhere higher than 50%, and especially noticeable in the RSA, but the dependence on Zaire for cobalt is the same. To a lesser degree the US depends upon Botswana, Zimbabwe, Gabon and Zambia.

These facts explain to a certain degree the support given to the RSA, but also the privileged relations with Nigeria. Carter had wished to make this state into one of the poles of stability in the region by favouring the installation of a 'Pax Nigeriana'. American businessmen consider this country as the only African market worthy of the name (after the RSA, of course). They base their opinion on the high density of the population, which obliges the state to reinforce its economic development (financed by oil), and on its political option in favour of economic liberalism.

The fact that America is so indebted to Nigeria has allowed this state to take clear-cut positions on the question of Namibia in opposition to the policy of Reagan. This proves that relations of economic interdependence could favour a greater independence of the African states with respect to the position taken by America.

But political and economic analyses are often contradictory . . . According to a letter giving confidential information to the Chase Manhattan Bank, the economy of Angola could be stabilized in view of a new start. Besides its riches in oil and diamonds, a liberal investment code and a policy of sound management are attracting more and more foreign firms. Gulf Oil is also doing its best to persuade the American government to establish diplomatic relations with this country. Recent facts seem to confirm that pragmatism is beginning to raise its voice, the spokesman of this tendency being George Schultz.

This picture of the different elements which make up American economic policy would be incomplete without a mention of the role of the CIA. Every year, the CIA's Committee of Economic Information draws up an Economic Alert List (EAL) which indicates the questions on which the agents of the CIA and those of other government agencies should pursue their investigations in the field.

For the period from November 1981 to March 1982, the EAL suggested two lines of reflection for the African continent:

1) Raw materials (oil and minerals, especially from southern Africa)
2) The governing teams in Africa.

Economic investigation here joins political reflection.

It is on the basis of an analysis by the CIA, which makes Nigeria the weakest link in the OPEC chain, that the American petrol companies have ceased to buy their crude oil from this country. They hoped to force it to price its oil lower than the OPEC tariff, which was $34 a barrel. This caused a considerable drop in the country's revenue and weakened its economy to a point which is not unconnected with the expulsion of two million workers, mostly from Ghana and the Cameroons, who were simply sent back to their own countries.

This policy brings with it unequal development, the impact of which is made harsher by the selective and even arbitrary nature of American food aid. Only 10% of this is destined to reach the Least Developed Countries (LDCs). The greater part goes to future clients of the US and is used as an instrument of economic and even military penetration. If any disagreement arises between the American government and the receiver state, the assistance is withdrawn. This was notably the case for Mozambique, but it also happened to a certain number of countries which protested too clearly against the support given by Washington to Savimbi (in Angola).

The last American instrument of pressure, and not the least, is the role which this imperialist power plays in the International Monetary Fund and notably in the Group of Ten. Agreements or the refusal of loans will again be used as the carrot or the stick.

Conclusion

Even if the American position seems to have undergone slight changes of late, it is nevertheless a fact that the political and strategic interests of this country bring with them economic effects as well as alliances and dissensions which have a direct influence on the lot of African populations and are among the causes which explain why they leave home.

And the re-election of Reagan scarcely allows us to hope for a break in the clouds which hang over American relations with Africa.

In the framework of the confrontation between east and west, the United States will continue to increase its military strength on the African continent and in the Indian Ocean (Diego Garcia) in order to control the strategic routes for oil and mineral supplies. The links with the RSA will be strengthened, although the swing of American public opinion against the regime of apartheid is a new factor which may well oblige the Reagan administration to modify its attitude.

Still more important than this intensification of Reagan's hard line could prove to be the 'solidarity' which the United States means to foster on the level of foodstuffs, by the introduction of ultra-liberal methods. They are aiming at a total and unrestricted opening of the African market to American goods, in fact a more or less elegant way of disposing of their agricultural surplus while, at the same time, ruining the African cultivation of staple foods.

This penetration can be considered as a source of anxiety when it is known that a memorandum to the State Department in 1983 recommended:

- to encourage the African and . . . American private sector to take a greater part in African agricultural development;

- to have recourse to direct assistance for private producers and to set up the mechanisms of free exchange;

- to favour a closer collaboration between the International Monetary Fund, the World Bank and private donors.

This 'free exchange' policy, accompanied by a subsidy of $500 million over five years, is a confirmation of the American offensive in Africa. Having recovered from its 'Vietnamese complex', the United States is ready to conquer the continent, repeating the well-known principle that what is good for America is good for Africa. Indeed the direct economic effects on the populations of Africa present a danger!

5. The Responsibility of the USSR

It is not easy to speak of the responsibility of the USSR in the production of refugees as, unlike France, Great Britain, Portugal and Germany, it is one of the few European countries which has no colonial history in Africa.

Since 1917, the USSR has never ceased to proclaim its moral, political and material support for movements of national liberation, always attaching it to Lenin's thesis on capitalism and imperialism. We can quote as examples of his opinion: 'The revolutionary movement of the peoples of the East can only develop successfully today and eventually succeed in relation to the revolutionary struggle of our Soviet republic against international imperialism.'[1] Or again: 'We will employ all our efforts to approach the Mongols, the Persians, the Indians, the Egyptians and join with them; we consider that it is both our duty and our interest to do so . . . We will try to accord a disinterested cultural assistance (to use the fine expression of the Polish social-democrats) to those peoples who are less advanced and more seriously oppressed than we, which means that we shall help them to learn how to use machines, make their work easier and pass over to democracy and socialism.'[2]

It is on the basis of this postulate that the USSR was to get involved in the struggle for independence of the countries more or less dominated by colonial powers, and the Soviet Union was directed along this path by Lenin's advisers on this question: Roy, an Indian, and Padmore, from Jamaica. After Lenin's death they had both broken off their relations with Stalin by 1927, but without ceasing to belong to their local national movement for ideological reasons linked up with the problems of the struggle for national liberation.

The first independence movement to come to power was in Ghana. The Convention People's Party (CPP) was a national front in which the bourgeoisie was dominant: its leader, Kwame N'Krumah, was a militant Marxist of Pan-African inspiration. Not only did he desire the victory of a socialist movement in his own country; he also wished to liberate the whole continent, and the states which were born of this movement were to unite under a federal government of socialist or socializing inspiration. On the diplomatic level, this tactic was not approved by the Soviets, although it received the approval of the Chinese. It is likely that at the time the Soviets were prejudiced against it by the failure of the world revolutionary movement in the Congo, where western imperialism had used the UN to introduce chaos.

We would suggest that the world movement for revolution, and its present leader, the USSR, were not ready at the time to accept the entry on the international scene of the African countries. As the movement becomes more pronounced, it will be centred around three principal questions:

1) How can the defence of the young democracies be assured against the imperialism of the former colonial powers?
2) How can the countries who have chosen socialism be helped to develop economically?
3) How can the coherence of the international revolutionary movement be assured, now that there are two large socialist powers?

In answer to the first question: the system of armament in use in Russia in the early 1950s was of limited efficacy, as the Soviets gave more importance to conventional armament of a classical type. At the same time, a sanitary cordon of more than 200 NATO military bases had been established against the USSR in neighbouring countries, and other systems of defence existed, such as ANZUS (Australia, New Zealand, and the United States), ASEAN (Australia, Thailand, the Philippines, Pakistan, France and the US), and CENTO (Central Treaty Organization), also known as the Pact of Baghdad (Great Britain, Iraq and Turkey). It was only after 1953, and despite all this, that the USSR was able to leave the closed field of defensive military action (to protect the national territory and the countries of the Warsaw Pact) and take up a firm political position in Africa of providing diversified assistance to national liberation movements. The ideological coloration of these movements can be very varied: the USSR has supported the African Independence Party of Guinea-Bissau and Cape Verde (PAIGC), the Popular Movement for the Independence of Angola (MPLA), the Revolutionary Front for the Liberation of Mozambique (FRELIMO), the South West African People's Organization (SWAPO), the African National Congress (ANC), the Algerian Front of National Liberation (FLN) and the Union of the Peoples of the Cameroons (UPC). But it steadfastly ignores all movements which bear the mark of Maoist ideology.

Nevertheless, the USSR has respected article 31 of the OAU concerning the inviolability of African frontiers, and supported all the resolutions and declarations of this organization on the struggle against colonialism, neo-colonialism and apartheid. The western countries have not done as much, except on those rare occasions when such a course coincides with their interests. Up to now, these countries have not broken their economic ties with the system of apartheid and continue to keep up their relations with this regime which is responsible for the flight of innumerable refugees.

Today several million Blacks have been chased from the so-called White zones to the Bantustans. Thousands of young students, workers and trade unionists have taken refuge in neighbouring countries. But South Africa continues to receive the respect of the western world thanks to her powerful economic system.

As far as the second question is concerned, the principles which govern Soviet help are incontestably correct: according to the Minister for Foreign Affairs of Pakistan, it is clear, when socialist countries give assistance, that:

● the rate of interest for loans is half that demanded by western countries;

● these countries generally give assistance, not to the branches of industry which produce consumer goods, but to those which furnish productive material, as for example steelworks and power stations, as these are in each country the base of industrialization;

● the loans accorded by socialist countries can be paid back either in kind, by the firms to which they were made, or by raw materials produced by the developing country in favour of which they were made.

The problem is that whereas the USSR was able to furnish working metallurgical complexes, as in Algeria, it is unable, for example, to supply agro-industrial plant.

Goods produced in the USSR are of poor quality and often ill-adapted to African conditions, and the USSR, which gives assistance on an exchange basis, finds it difficult to accept large quantities of privately consumed produce such as cocoa, peanuts and coffee, which its industry is unable to transform. The solution adopted is a three-cornered trade operation: the produce is delivered to capitalist countries in exchange for strong currency. The socialist countries find it hard to accept the means of payment proposed by some of the new countries, the cocoa from Ghana and the coffee from Angola, while others can pay in kind and make profitable exchanges with the socialist countries, which possess the means of storage and processing. This, for example, is the case for Cuba, which pays with sugar, and for Egypt, which offers cotton. President Nasser once declared: 'Last winter, we only had corn reserves for a month and we lacked oil. At the same time, we wanted to sell our cotton. We asked for help from the Americans, who refused. But the Russians sold us corn and oil and bought our cotton. They allowed us to survive and to avoid western domination.'

In fact, young states who wish to free themselves from the stranglehold of the dollar can choose between only two alternatives: adapt their production so as to fit into COMECON or possess a product which can be converted into strong currency. This is the case for metals, precious stones or oil, and it allows them to build up an economic sovereignty which contributes to their harmonious development.

Many African countries, progressive or not, have found themselves confronted with this dilemma, which has been the principal cause of the rise of unstable political systems or of economic and social regression. The capitalist countries show that they are not in favour of the industrial development of the Third World and pay less and less for its produce. The socialist countries, and most of all the USSR, are often charged with complicity when leaders in Africa, or elsewhere in the Third World, try to obtain a true independence, but all they can offer is a system of integration, with all the advantages that this affords — and the limits it imposes.

All this makes it more difficult to manage the economy and creates factors of unrest. All the countries which are not constantly threatened with troubles produce oil or precious metals (Libya, Algeria and Zimbabwe). The others, which have to face economic difficulties, receive only slight assistance from the socialist countries. Military aid is of the first importance to maintain national sovereignty, but is by itself insufficient to assure prosperity. If these young African nations are to engage in economic development free from the control of multinational firms, they need a plan for general economic assistance as well. We have seen that the USSR and the socialist countries are for the moment unable to provide this. The result is the multiplication of military putsches and interventions in different parts of Africa organized by the countries of the Atlantic Alliance; the result is also famine (for example in Ethiopia). We shall see later that the inadequacy of the assistance given to the countries who engage in a non-capitalist form of development is fatal to their political regimes as well as being one of the main sources of refugees.

At the start, the USSR won prestige with the help it offered the young African states, but it lost its influence because it lacked effective technological means.

In answer to the third question, it should be clearly affirmed that the split of the workers' movement into two antagonistic blocs has been, for more than 20 years, one of the most dangerous causes of imbalance for the liberation movements of the young independent countries. The leaders of the parties or fronts or movements of liberation have spent their time tearing one another to pieces in the name of two leaders: Moscow and Peking.

In 1965 a third leader came to the fore after the famous Tricontinental Conference at Havana, where the leaders of all the liberation movements and the progressive parties met together. Cuba's bid for leadership was backed up by the camp of the non-aligned countries, but met with little support from the two socialist giants, who hardly appreciated the initiative. Indeed, backed only by the non-aligned group, it was largely wishful thinking as far as the liberation of Third World countries was concerned.

These contradictions, kept alive within the international revolutionary movement which was supposedly behind the liberation movements fuelled local quarrels which often ended in a manner tragic for the people. At the time the USSR was heavily responsible for these tragedies, because she was unable to find any solution for this disunity among parties who all defended more or less the same aims and had the same interests.

The tragic situations created by the failure to answer these three questions were to be at the heart of events which brought with them a new flow of refugees.

In 1956 Nasser, with the full support of the socialist world, was to involve Egypt in a dynamic and ambitious plan of development. Industrialization was underway, but despite enormous aid from the USSR, Egypt was unable to overcome her underdevelopment. The assistance furnished by Russia concerned primarily heavy industry and the domain of the army, but the social sector was badly neglected. This provoked the flight of thousands of opposition militants, working men and trained personnel, from 1956 until today. Egypt has been freed from the colonial yoke and has received substantial help, which has benefited the well-to-do classes above all, but she has been unable to create the ideal conditions for development. The worst hit victims were the Egyptian communists, who took refuge in their thousands in the neighbouring countries.

In 1957 Ghana acceded to independence. The leader of the country chose socialism and appealed first of all to the USSR and to China, asking for a plan of development which would make the country less dependent. The antagonism between China and the USSR was to be one of the main causes of the military putsch against the progressive regime in 1966, when the country was beginning to stabilize the economy, freed from the clutches of transnational corporations involved in cocoa, gold, etc. Hundreds were to flee their country; even today Ghana is still wounded by social and political movements caused by a lack of solidarity behind its government.

In 1958 Sekou Touré obliged a reticent colonial power (France) to recognize the national sovereignty of his country. Guinea received from the USSR various forms of assistance which allowed the country to keep on its course from 1958 to 1961, but France surrounded the country with an economic, political and ideological blockade which eventually broke her government. Thousands of economic refugees left the country for Senegal, Mali, the Ivory Coast, Sierra Leone and Liberia. Guinea had lost her trade with the neighbouring countries, and the assistance furnished by the Soviets was insufficient to take their place. Faced by a collapse, Sekou Touré found no other way to resolve his problems than a series of cruel repressions which caused the death of several hundreds of militants of his own Democratic Party of Guinea (PDG). There are more than 500,000 refugees from Guinea in Senegal. Decisive for their flight was the fact that Soviet assistance was both insufficient and inappropriate to the situation, and that the leaders of the PDG lacked political maturity.

1960 was the date of the independence of Congo-Leopoldville, under a national liberation movement headed by Patrice Lumumba. The exploitation of the mines was a strategic necessity for the economy of the capitalist countries and, faced with the strength and the determination of Congolese nationalism, the directors of the mining companies obliged the industrial region of Katanga to proclaim its secession. The hesitant intervention of the UN, at this time controlled by American diplomacy, aggravated the political situation and provoked a civil war which set the whole country on fire.

Thousands of refugees settled in the neighbouring states or wandered like nomads throughout the country. The NATO powers discredited the nationalists and treated them as communist agents. The only countries on their side were those of the socialist and non-aligned blocs, and they had the support of the progressive countries in Africa (Tanzania, Egypt, Guinea and Ghana), as well as the humanitarian movements of democratic states.

The USSR only gives diplomatic assistance, mainly at the UN level, as well as charitable aid to certain nationalists, rivalling in this the activities of China in other places.

The nationalists lost their hold on the Congo, and NATO put its candidate at the head of the state administration after several episodes of civil war in 1965. The Congolese peoples paid a very heavy price to see the end of their calvary, if not of their poverty, for poverty has been on the increase in Zaire ever since. Today, the transnational corporations dealing in copper and precious metals have pillaged the riches of the country. The International Monetary Fund (IMF) is installed on the spot, but can find no solution to the economic, political and social crisis which rocks the country.

In 1977 the National Front for the Liberation of the Congo (FNLC), formed of former Katanga policemen, after helping the MPLA to liberate Angola, rose against the government of Mobutu and occupied the Shaba (Katanga). Faced with their successes and the capitulation of the Shaba, NATO called in the forces of its allies (Egypt, Morocco, and France) and the rebels beat a retreat. A savage repression was undertaken against the population, which caused the flight into Angola and Zambia of thousands of the inhabitants, swelling the already large number of Zairese exiles. The operation was renewed in the following year, and the number of refugees continued to grow.

Today the Zairese refugee is a legendary figure, far beyond the frontiers of Africa. The Soviets are chiefly responsible for the two incidents of civil war, but they prefer to keep silent and refuse to react. If they had given the refugees anything like the assistance furnished by NATO to the government of Mobutu, the course of history would have been different.

In 1971 some progressive Sudanese officers, in sympathy with the Sudanese Communist Party, prepared a putsch against General Nimeiry. They failed, thanks to the effective military assistance furnished by the Libyan President Gadhafi. Thousands of the leaders and militants of the party were arrested and judged by a summary procedure; secretary-general Magdjoub was executed. Sudan had become one of the closest allies of the US, but this did not put a stop to its co-operation with the USSR, which restricted its action to diplomatic protests, but refused to undertake any retaliation. Thousands of refugees fled to Ethiopia, to Egypt and to the Middle East.

The situation remained precarious in Sudan under the iron rod of General Nimeiry, despite the amnesty accorded thirteen years later to 13,000 political prisoners. With all their leaders in hiding or living in exile, the political organizations of Sudan will take a long time to recover.

In 1977 war broke out between Somalia, a firm ally of the Soviets in the Horn of Africa, and her huge neighbour Ethiopia, for the possession of the Ethiopian region of Ogaden. This war and the ongoing struggle waged by the EPLF in Eritrea against a military central government still in the throes of the revolutionary excitement which followed the fall of Emperor Haile Selassie, suddenly revealed to international public opinion the existence of a national problem in Ethiopia.

The result was a double reversal of her alliances by the USSR: first of all, the alliance with Somalia, which the USSR had considered until then as a friendly country, and then with respect to the EPLF, which had counted on the support of the USSR and the socialist countries. Somalia was to invade the Ogaden in a lightning campaign, in violation of article 431 of the OAU which stipulates the inviolability of former colonial frontiers. Confronted with this dilemma, the USSR gave her full support to Ethiopia, who chased the invaders from the Ogaden with the help of Cuban soldiers.

This led to more than a million people taking refuge in Somalia and in Djibouti. Looking back at the situation we can see that the USSR was more sensitive to her geo-political interests in face of the NATO powers and their allies (Egypt, Saudi Arabia, Israel and Iran) than to the interests of the people of Ethiopia and Somalia, on whose governments she could have brought considerable influence to bear, be it on the material or on the political and ideological level. As far as Eritrea is concerned, the tragedy continues and the number of refugees is increasing in Sudan, without counting the people of Tigre who are running away from the war.

At the time of the Ethiopian revolution, the USSR could have helped, by means of diplomatic pressure and with the help of friendly African countries, to resolve the antagonism between the two countries, and even perhaps to find a solution to the Eritrean tragedy despite the fanaticism of the leaders on both sides.

In 1975 Angola obtained her independence and chose the socialist camp. South Africa immediately invaded the country, crossing through Namibia, massacring the people and ravaging everything in its path with heavy bombing. The Popular Movement for the Liberation of Angola (MPLA) appealed to Cuba, who sent troops without delay, as did Guyana, Guinea and Nigeria, with the tacit approval of the OAU. Nearly 20,000 Cubans were thrown into the battle and pushed the South Africans back to the frontier of Namibia.

The RSA has always insisted that the condition *sine qua non* under which she will grant Namibia her independence, in accordance with resolution no. 435 of the Security Council of the UN, is the departure of Cuban forces from Angola. In 1985 the Cubans were still in Angola. On 20 March 1984, Castro and Eduardo Dos Santos, the President of Angola, published a communiqué announcing the conditions of the Cuban withdrawal. But this first step runs the risk of having no further consequences, faced with the bad faith of the RSA, which refuses to apply the Lusaka agreements. Faced also with the growing influence of Jonas Savimbi, who is supported by the RSA and the US, and who is beginning to reap the fruits of the discontent of the populations obliged to flee the zones of conflict and suffering the jolts of an economy disorganized by the interventions of the RSA and the errors of the MPLA.

And the USSR? Of course Dos Santos expresses his gratitude for the economic, political and military assistance he has received from Moscow. But it is difficult to see why the USSR waited until 1983 to train the soldiers of the MPLA to counterattack in a guerrilla war, when UNITA had been using those methods for a long time. It looks as if Moscow wanted to force Luanda to be more orthodox, to 'flirt' less openly with the western powers on the economic level. It is indeed well known that Angola and Mozambique have been thinking of joining the group of the African, Caribbean and Pacific powers (ACP) and signing the Convention of Lomé. That would be a way of breaking the isolation to which their membership of the socialist camp has condemned them.

But for the intervention of the Cubans, there is no doubt that the RSA would have transformed the whole region into a battle zone, while the Soviets would have sacrificed their strategic help to geo-political considerations, to the detriment of the independence and national sovereignty of Angola. There are many examples where the Soviets have put their national interests before their political and ideological duty. We cannot quote all of them.

Conclusion

The policy of peaceful coexistence practised by the USSR with respect to the capitalist countries has not always proved an asset to the liberation movements in Africa and has not always been well understood.

The internationalism paraded since 1917 has given way to a policy which seeks to develop sophisticated military weapons, on land, at sea and in the air, in an attempt to catch up with the US and the other NATO powers. For the same reason the Soviet fleet has spread out all over the world, often getting the better of NATO forces.

That is why every attempt to build up a regime desirous of justice and progress is immediately compared to the construction of a communist regime. The nationalists of the African National Congress (ANC) in South Africa, the South West African People's Organization (SWAPO) in Namibia, the Polisario in the Western Sahara, as well as those who oppose the regime in Zaire, are all assimilated to international terrorists in the view of American theorists such as Henry Kissinger, Zbigniew Brzezinski or Caspar Weinberger.

Nationalists and progressive thinkers in Africa do not consider the USSR as an imperialist power in the sense in which Lenin has defined this term. They are aware of the power of its ideology and take account of this at every point in their struggle. At the present time only the socialist countries favour the political independence and economic development of Africa, but the continent is mainly situated in the sphere of influence of capitalist countries. Only 2% of the world's trade with Third World countries are made with the socialist bloc, and in these exchanges the military sector holds a predominant place, followed by the sale of means of production. They also grant university scholarships to Africans and send out technicians on the basis of co-operation, for in these domains the socialist countries are second to none.

It goes without saying that in the matter of development, the socialist countries are no longer everybody's first choice. The young African states, even if they have progressive ideas, turn more and more towards the capitalist countries when they need assistance to develop their industries. As economic and political causes are at the heart of the debate about how to envisage the refugee problem, it is clear that the stream of refugees will not dry up until the states which provide technology and armaments feel really concerned by the debate on the future of Africa. And today it is clear that the African nationalist movements, whose struggle produces a large number of refugees because of the repression to which they are submitted, are only supported by the countries of Northern Europe, the humanitarian movements, and the socialist countries under the leadership of the USSR.

Notes

1. Lenin, *Complete Works*, vol. 30 (Paris and Moscow), p. 149.
2. Ibid., vol. 23, p. 73.

6. France's Policy in Africa

The Project of de Gaulle

The French Fifth Republic was a regime of personal power supported by the right wing. How then did it succeed so quickly in decolonizing Black Africa, whereas the Fourth Republic, far more under the influence of the left, always remained obstinately opposed to the very idea? No doubt de Gaulle had a plan which was an essential element of his domestic policy: the colonies were to pass from a regime of direct domination to a neo-colonial regime, preserving all the value transfers that profited the big firms and part of the French middle classes. The plan was pragmatic, and not merely a 'grand design' built up after the defeat in Indochina and when he was caught up in the quagmire of the Algerian war.

After granting independence to a number of countries in the 1960s, certain measures were to be taken to assure the success of this policy: bilateral agreements were to prolong the privileged links with France and guarantee French interests; the CFA franc was to be kept in the monetary zone of the French franc. The guarantee of the Bank of France and its institutional mechanisms made this zone a simple extension of the French economic area. This was a major advantage for French investors: practically no risk was taken in the exchange, and the freedom accorded to financial transfers allowed French firms in Africa to send their profits home without difficulty. In addition, the currency brought in by those countries who were members of the Community supported the value of the franc.

The countries which accept these dispositions are free from certain monetary worries: they enjoy a relative currency stability and a system of banks of issue which is not at the mercy of the local government's dictates. On the other hand they do not really possess a national currency, and are unable to use it as an arm in times of crisis.

Sending advisers to these countries will also play a powerful role. It is difficult to estimate the impact they have on the wider economic and political options of the countries they assist, but it is none the less certain that these Frenchmen contribute, often unconsciously, to maintaining the cultural, technical and political hold of the former colonial power. It should be noted in passing that France is one of the countries which demands that the advisers be housed and paid by the states that receive them.

But there is worse than that. These dispositions have proved insufficient in the struggle against progressive mass movements in Africa, which have succeeded in overthrowing the governments set up to facilitate neo-colonial co-operation. When its problems in Africa became serious, the French government did not hesitate to encourage or at least cover up political assassinations or the overthrowing of heads of state. Among the victims were Sylvanus Olympio in Togo (1963), Léon M'Ba at Libreville (1964), Ben Barka in Paris in 1965, and David Dacko in the Central African Republic in 1966.

When it is not considered either necessary or advisable to take such measures, corruption is used. This is a sore point for African governments, as it is not only a means of dominating the men in power by using their desire for riches, but it also provides a market for French luxury exports and offers safe deposits in foreign banks which are still in the French monetary zone.

Giscard Goes on Safari

The aim of French politics — to keep the door to Africa open for French and western interests — has not changed since decolonization, but the way in which this policy has been conducted has gone from bad to worse.

De Gaulle had a grand design for Africa, completing his vision of the greatness of France; there was a logical consistency in his thought and the way he used the ideas of 1789 made it appear generous. By avoiding the strong grasp of the great powers he helped the young states, for a time at least, to join the non-aligned powers.

Pompidou concealed this ambition and maintained, for better or for worse, a co-operation based on the defence of France's economic interests. Giscard claimed to be realistic, but his undertakings were often tactless and unreasonable, and his greed for the riches of Africa was often doubled by capricious feelings of resentment, even if this defeated the principal aims of his policy (examples of this are the Western Sahara and Chad). At the outset of his term as president, Giscard tried to make Africa his private hunting ground, thus braving the threats of the Soviets and sometimes at the cost of selling off to the USA certain fields formerly reserved, like the health services.

To side-track people, all his enterprises were accompanied by reassuring humanitarian speeches, which nevertheless failed to deceive either the African peoples or, for that matter, the rest of the world. The African continent was less frequently considered as destined to evolve normally towards a policy of non-alignment, which needed to be encouraged by mutual co-operation undertaken to the advantage of both sides. It was seen more and more as a chosen ground to perpetuate western interests. Every kind of means, from corruption to direct military intervention, was to be used to realize this policy. The African people would continue to pay the bill for all these upheavals by flight and depopulation.

When he came to power in 1974, Giscard inherited three military brigades stationed on African territory. At the end of his seven years' presidency, the intervention force in Africa counted several divisions, including parachute troops, marine light infantry, airborne troops and a detachment of shock troops. This was the setting for the clumsy intervention in the Western Sahara in 1977, the result of which was the fall of Ould Daddah in July 1978, the isolation of Morocco at the OAU and the quarrel between Algeria and France.

In Chad, a disorderly answer was given to a confused situation: theoretically, the operation was destined to restrain the excesses of Gadhafi and punish General Malloum who, in April 1975, had overthrown Tombalbaye, the former protégé of the French government, and expelled the French troops. The kidnapping of Madame Claustre by Hissen Habré gave the French government an opportunity to negotiate with him and propose a ransom. French troops could appear in the country again, and Hissen Habré became the Prime Minister of his former rival, General Malloum, whom he sent into exile seven months later.

But Hissen Habré was unable to keep the situation in hand and, with the help of Gadhafi, Goukouni Oueddei took his place and threw the French troops out in March 1980. Up to the end Giscard had backed the wrong horse and reinforced Libyan influence, while giving the African countries reasons to disapprove of him. And during all this time, every time the head of state changed, new columns of refugees set out on the road.

Giscard took a similar stand in Central Africa. When, after the massacre of the schoolchildren in 1979, the corrupt emperor Bokassa became too openly embarrassing, Giscard took advantage of his absence to overthrow him and put in his place David Dacko, who had been chased from power 14 years earlier. He paid no attention to Ange Patassé, who had better claims to represent the aspirations of the people, nor to Abel Goumba, who was a friend of the socialists.

Up to this point Giscard was apparently working alone, but things were to become more involved. The intervention of Kolwezi has not been forgotten in Zaire. it was accompanied by a lot of noisy advertising and a call on the patriotic spirit, but it is now clear that Giscard was nothing more on this occasion than the lackey of western imperialism. If he was not playing this role, how are we to explain that in 1977 the French took the place of Carter, to whom Mobutu had appealed but who was unable to accept for reasons of internal policy (the Americans were still reeling from the shock of their defeat in Vietnam)? Why was US air transport used in 1978? Why were French troops sent to the Lebanon in the summer of

1978 wearing the blue helmet of the UN, and why was this announced in English on American territory? When Giscard proclaimed, just after the intervention at Kolwezi: 'France takes her responsibilities in Africa and acts on her own account', the prevarication was a little heavy-handed. The truth was that the Trilateral Commission had given France the responsibility to act in Africa with the help of American logistics.

Under Giscard, technical co-operation and bilateral assistance have increased considerably. French personnel in Africa represent about 30% of the total number of foreigners in the continent, and account for 23,000 individuals, most of whom are teachers. The countries to which aid personnel are sent must answer to evident economic and political standards: most of the funds go to the Cameroons, Gabon, Ivory Coast and Senegal. By a strange coincidence, after the fall of Bokassa, French advisers entered the administration of the Central African Republic in large numbers and now occupy decision-making posts.

It is well known that Africa has massive reserves of raw materials, many of which are still unexploited. Uranium reserves (to be found in Gabon, Niger and Namibia) have a special importance for building up the new type of sub-imperialism which Giscard coveted for France. The possession of uranium makes it easier to restructure French industrial capital and allows France to play a leading role in the nuclear industry, decisive from the point of view of energy and military power.

Before turning the page after more than 20 years of government by the right, a last word should be said about the action of the secret services which have contributed to political unrest in Africa since the end of the Second World War. France is not the only power to manipulate hidden strings, and the rivalries between the services are well known. But we should remember that one of the most murderous tragedies, that of Biafra, was the direct result of the work of the Service of Foreign Documentation and of Counter-Espionage (SDECE), as well as that of Foccart's network, then an ally of the Portuguese International Police for the Defence of the State (PIDE). France wanted the oil in the eastern part of Nigeria, and she was ready to stir up a secession to get it. Nigerian troops armed by the British, Americans and the Soviets were to crush the attempt in a bath of blood. The terrible dramas which resulted from this effort at destabilization, and the number of refugees who fled because of it, are still vivid in people's memories.

Ten years' intervention in Chad ended in a civil war between the different factions of the National Front for the Liberation of Chad (FROLINAT); this war caused more exile, suffering and death.

Generally, be it a hidden effect or a goal openly sought by the government, the neo-colonial domination of France has either supported African politicians who had no deep concern for the basic development of their peoples, or undermined the political order in whole regions with the risk of breaking her alliances . . . In both cases, the consequences for refugees were heavy.

Hopes Raised in May 1981

The election of François Mitterrand to the presidency of the French Republic aroused as much enthusiasm among the peoples of Africa as in France. One could reasonably wonder if France was equipped to live up to these expectations. The plan of the socialists proclaimed that 'the honour and the interest of the country demanded that she take the opposite course' to that which had been followed up to then. Was a commercial capitalism under the influence of the transnational corporations going to give way to an industrial and agricultural development which would exploit the riches of the African countries for the good of their inhabitants?

Africa was not unknown territory for Mitterrand: he was Minister of the Overseas Departments in 1950 and 1951; he had kept up close relations with Houphouët Boigny and Senghor, and the latter also belonged to the Second Socialist International. His first declarations showed concern for the Third World, a respect for human rights and disapproval of dictatorships.

The new government started work with two visits by Guy Penne, who was responsible for African Affairs at the Elysée in June and August 1981. The nomination of Jean-Pierre Cot as Minister for Co-operation, and the declarations he made when he took up office, had a deep significance, as he affirmed his intention to decolonize co-operation and put an end to racial discrimination in Africa. It is not surprising that South Africa felt a little worried. Socialist France, however, decided to honour the promises made before 10 May.

As a target for 1985 the new government chose to give, as assistance to the Third World, the 0.7% of GNP decided on by the UN, and in 1982, without including the Departments and Territories Overseas (DOM/TOM) which had up to then been counted in the Third World and received the lion's share of this assistance, they increased the sum assigned to it by 24% and guaranteed that it would be directed towards projects which were perhaps less 'profitable', but which were certainly better adapted to the needs of the countries which received them.

On the other hand, the ambition of the Ministries of Co-operation and Foreign Affairs is to open up French-speaking Africa and extend French assistance and also French influence to all the countries of the Third World, especially the English-speaking countries of Africa. This breakthrough in the direction of the English-speaking countries is in fact a new interpretation of the effort started under the preceding presidency.

The wound caused by the fact that de Gaulle had taken the side of Biafra was partly healed and the penetration of Nigeria had been able to start under Giscard. Now France was free to take a growing part in one of the first countries in Africa. Nigeria became a partner second only to Algeria, and France's third furnisher of oil, which represents 96% of

Nigeria's exports to France and the principal part of French imports from English-speaking countries.

French firms are particularly active in the field of construction and engineering: 26 are actually engaged in development projects, of which we can quote from memory Bouygues, Renault, Dumez and Fougerolles. Sofrerail is to superintend the building of the railway from Port Harcourt to Ajokuta. In collaboration with the Japanese firm Marubeni Hitachi, Bouygues is building a thermal power station at Lagos. In all, more than 120 firms are working in the country in concert with Nigerian firms.

Another spectacular advance is that made by the banks through their branches: the National Bank of Paris is affiliated to the United Bank of Africa, the leading bank in the country. The International Bank for West Africa holds fifth place, and the Société Générale is becoming more solidly established every day. France also furnishes technical assistance by means of a training programme for students, in France or in Nigeria.

France is also making an 'assault' on the former Portuguese colonies. The plan was developed at Lisbon at the end of 1981 by Mitterrand and Eanes. It is tolerated by Washington, but Moscow rightly has some misgivings as the aim of the scheme is to bring Western Europe back in full force in the territories which had fallen under Marxist influence.

Portugal feels that her former colonies are disappointed by their collaboration with the countries of the Soviet bloc, and wish to offset their relations with Moscow by creating new links with the west. They would like to enter into the Africa-Caribbean-Pacific group (ACP) which is linked to the EEC by the Convention of Lomé. This explains why these countries are progressively reversing their alliances and returning to their former masters.

But Portugal has no money to spare and her technology is as yet ill adapted, so she turns to France as the former colonial power in the best position to co-operate with her. That is how Mitterrand is to extend French influence to Guinea-Bissau, Mozambique, the Cape Verde, signing agreements on co-operation, sending medical and agricultural assistance in the form of 7,000 tons of corn, maize and other cereals to Sâo Tome, Cape Verde, Mozambique and Guinea-Bissau, and supplying direct financial aid to Angola. These countries urgently need electrification, modernization of the agricultural sector and a transfer of appropriate technology; asked to furnish help in these sectors sufficiently advantageous in comparison to that offered by Cuba and the USSR, Portugal was at a loss, but France was able to offer her services. We can nevertheless wonder if the Soviets will accept the loss of their leadership in these sensitive regions, and we should not forget the irritation of some small countries like Cape Verde, who have hardly been consulted on these geo-political manoeuvres, but who do not agree to being treated like children, with no say in the matter when their guardian is changed.

The agreement on Algerian gas is presented as exemplary: a contract signed in 1981 at a higher price allows Algeria to be better paid. The

Algerian government considers the price as just, because it allows the gas therm to be evaluated at the same level as the oil therm. In other words, France has given a concrete application of the valorization of raw materials. The French government regarded it as a case of assistance in the form of the correct valorization of a product: the cost is to be borne by the budget of public assistance and subtracted from the total amount set aside for assistance to developing countries. This makes it appear as a significant gesture towards Algeria, with whom France wants to restore good relations, rather than a great open gesture embracing all other Third World countries. But is France able to indulge in such a gesture?

At the start, the change of government in France appeared encouraging for Namibia: the South West African People's Organization (SWAPO) was at last authorized to open an office in Paris. In the Contact Group,[1] Claude Cheysson was to use his influence in favour of UN Resolution no. 435 for the independence of Namibia, to fight against the unyielding attitude adopted by America since the election of Reagan, and demand that a precise calendar be established for decolonization. France banned the investment of public funds in South Africa and discouraged private investments.

But as time goes on, France has become more circumspect. Claude Cheysson had announced that his country will retire from the Contact Group if the USA refuses to change its attitude. The US has made no changes — but France was still a member of the group in early 1983.

Sam Nujoma complained recently that France was playing a double game:

> We appreciated the affirmation made by Mr. Mauroy in September before the General Assembly of the UN, that his country was opposed to the idea of 'linkage'.[2] But French technicians are still working in South Africa, helping to produce Panhard tanks and Mirage planes; France continues to deliver spare parts for the Alouettes, the Pumas and the Super-Frelons used by the racist government. We ask France to impose economic sanctions against Pretoria. Her declarations should be followed by practical actions.[3]

Socialist France, however, has decided to honour the contracts signed previously with South Africa. There are rumours of the delivery of a second nuclear power plant which was not on the books before May 1981, but different lobbies (among which is the Socialist Party) have provisionally persuaded the government not to proceed with this.

But we have to recognize that even if France did finally leave the Contact Group in 1984, she took no economic sanctions against Pretoria, and she failed to recognize the authority of the UN Council for Namibia,[4] as also that the SWAPO is the only party representative of the Namibian people.

In Mali, the French government has given the police the material necessary to equip flying security squads: 13 lorries, 20 motorcycles, a criminology laboratory and a radio network to allow the police stations in

Bamako to maintain permanent contact with one another. This seems a strange way in which to help a repressed people to shake off the yoke of a corrupt regime whose only interest is to get rich at the expense of the population.

Was it really necessary to go to Zaire 18 months after taking power? If Mitterrand delayed the meeting of the African heads of state for a year, he must have had a good reason for doing so: had these reasons disappeared in 1982?

And what is to be said of the sale of arms? Far from stopping, it is on the increase. French arms sales have grown twice as fast as France's other exports. France is aggressive on this point because she needs to guarantee the supplies of uranium necessary for her nuclear industry — without mentioning the balance of payments, which is seriously in danger at the moment.

If we add in economic decisions, like the effort to reconquer the home market and exclude Third World products, especially in the field of textiles, it is clear that the decision of Jean-Pierre Cot to decolonize the Ministry of Co-operation was neither popular nor effective.[5] In this light, his resignation in December 1982 appears as the logical consequence of this development.

Jean-Pierre Cot's Resignation: A Change of Course?

The press spoke of the defeat of idealism by pragmatic considerations, and it is tempting to accept striking formulations like this. But it would be more honest to look at the problem in greater detail.

It is true that Claude Cheysson, supporting firmly the ideology of the Brandt Commission and repeating the terms of the discourse given at Cancun (Mexico), has affirmed that the help given to the Third World must also bring an advantage to the developed countries: 'Who can still dream of relaunching economy in the developed countries without giving them markets? Who can survive today without exports? Helping the Third World is also helping oneself to get out of the crisis.' This is true, but Jean-Pierre Cot himself has often been torn between self-interested assistance, favouring French development, and a mutual form of assistance which profits both north and south. Didn't he himself say that 'it isn't easy to pass from rhetoric to politics'?[6]

Indeed, no practical follow-up was given to the proposal to create a Ministry of the Third World which would put all the developing countries on the same footing. French assistance remains essentially destined for the French-speaking African countries, it is bilateral, and the returns are still of the order of two-thirds of what is given. The Ministry of Co-operation is caught between the desire to finance projects which really respond to the needs of the countries concerned and the imperious necessity to offset a commercial balance which shows a heavy deficit.

The problems met in the field were exacerbated by the difficulties of relating to Jean-Pierre Cot. However good your intentions may be, you cannot change your policy with impunity. To refuse a loan to Gabon because it was destined to finance a polytechnical institution in the President's native village, or to refuse to deliver helicopters that had already been promised, will finally strain relations between two countries, because the decision is imposed by authority. And then Bongo, like the other heads of state in French-speaking Africa, had no intention of sharing his privileges, and did not appreciate the desire of the Minister for Co-operation to extend his assistance to the other countries of the Third World.

To all these reasons underlying the resignation of Jean-Pierre Cot we should add a few details of varying importance. First of all, the division of responsibilities between the Quai d'Orsay and the Ministry of Co-operation was not clearly defined. It has been suggested that Claude Cheysson wished to unite all cultural and diplomatic affairs under the authority of his ministry, and naturally it didn't please Jean-Pierre Cot to be left with only the technical dimension.

At the Elysée there were two sources of friction. Guy Penne, the Special Adviser on the Affairs of Africa and Madagascar, happened to belong to a Masonic Lodge opposed to two other Lodges which were pro-American. Guy Penne feels, and doubtless for good reasons, that if France does not look after her interests in Africa, the USA and the USSR will take advantage of the situation, but Jean-Pierre Cot did not agree with this analysis. Above all, Jean-Pierre Cot disapproved of the stranglehold of freemasonry on French co-operation. Strangely enough, the lodge to which Guy Penne belonged obtained the resignation of Senghor and Ahidjo at the end of 1982, and Jean-Pierre Cot's successor, Christian Nucci, is also a member of this lodge.

There were also direct disagreements with Mitterrand, who had sent out a mission to ask the heads of state in Africa to give up the single-party principle and to accept the existence of a social-democrat party guaranteed by Bonn and Paris. Jean-Pierre Cot probably agreed with the fundamental idea behind this policy, that it is impossible to change one's politics without changing one's partners, but he refused to admit supervision by Bonn and Paris.

The pressure of French interests in Africa should not be ignored.[7] This lobby is headed by Jacques Foccart, a retired company director in Gabon, well known under de Gaulle and Pompidou as the Elysée's special consultant on African and Malagasy affairs. He was one of the founders of the right-wing Service of Civil Action (SAC) and had organized, as we have already seen, various intelligence networks. His analysis was that of Guy Penne: if French imperialism walks out, the road is open to the United States and the USSR, and if Jean-Pierre Cot is given a free hand to organize social-democrat parties without a guarantee, and to give unconditional assistance, France risks upsetting the weak African powers under the pretext of changing partners too quickly.

So against the judgement of Jean-Pierre Cot, but with the support of Guy Penne and the French lobby in Africa, Mitterrand was to go and shake hands with Mobutu, whom he detests, and make a visit to Gabon, where Omar Bongo is rampant, but where Foccart is king.

And that is how French imperialism continues in Africa, despite the declarations made at Cancun.[8]

Conclusion

All this goes to prove that there is as yet no real change in French policy in Africa, and that none will be possible until it is part of the structural changes in Europe that the government is seeking to bring about.

Despite the declarations of Claude Cheysson, the speech of François Mitterrand at Cancun, and the position taken at Mexico in favour of El Salvador, policy towards the Third World does not yet appear as a priority. French politics cannot jeopardize the politics of the blocs, and the French have never taken a firmer stand in favour of the Atlantic Alliance. Faced with such facts, how can we build up a north–south policy based on non-alignment? As long as the Socialist Party fails to adopt an anti-imperialist strategy in the European context, how can we hope that France will make radical changes in her policy in Africa?

Has not France, even if under constraint, developed in Chad a policy which suits the United States? The final aim is different of course: the US wants to have a relay in Chad on the road to the Horn; France wants to preserve her traditional zone of influence in the region. For the moment she is the leading partner, but the regular meetings she has with the US aim at co-ordinating these policies. We can add in passing that this gives the US a right to look into French interests in Africa.

There is in the French attitude a mixture of complicity with the USA and a certain amount of opposition. Paris, for example, is fundamentally opposed to Washington on food policy. In agreement with the EEC, France wishes to develop a strategy of assistance aimed at the agricultural self-sufficiency of Africa and the development of small local industries and a policy of energy. France wishes to see an increase in the buying power of the African farmer, whereas the US, standing by its theory of comparative advantage on the international market, thinks that Africa should not live off her own produce but procure her food thanks to American exports.

These differences, like the harmony which exists between the two capitals, result from the opposition between the ideological discourse held in France and the country's economic interests, or better: the private interests of certain French lobbies, which exert a powerful influence on Franco-African relations. If France wants to put her national productivity to work again, she has to count on receiving raw materials from Africa, and so must deal tactfully with the governments in power.

Yet if a self-centred development is to become possible and be felt necessary, in Africa as in France, a new form of growth must be found. The supporters of the left are entangled in the contradictions which are inherent in their having assumed power in the middle of a capitalist system, and they are hedged in between the economic restrictions to be expected in a time of crisis and the bitter invectives of the right. They will not find it easy to act in accordance with the speeches they made before the elections. It is unhappily most likely that the African people will go on being chased about and harried, the unhappy victims of situations, manoeuvres and interests which take no account of them.

This is the context in which to understand the limits set upon France's intervention in the dramatic problem of African refugees, in Africa and elsewhere.

Notes

1. The task of the Contact Group is to facilitate negotiations to ensure the departure of South Africa from Namibia and to bring this country to independence. As well as France, Great Britain, West Germany, Canada and the United States are members.

2. South Africa wants to 'link' the departure of her troops from Namibia to that of the Cuban troops from Angola.

3. Interview accorded to *Le Monde* on 25 January 1983.

4. This organization was created in 1967 as the legal authority to guarantee the administration of the Namibian territory. But its authority is powerless because Great Britain, the United States and France constantly refuse it the right to take sanctions against the RSA.

5. He had hoped to encourage less structured projects, which would have brought less profit to the investing organizations but would have been better adapted to the needs of the countries for which they were destined, and to associate more closely the non-governmental organizations in the decisions of the government.

6. Statement made to *Le Monde* on 19 August 1981.

7. Among these we can quote: the Mills of Corbeil, the French Company for the Development of Textiles (CFDT) in Chad, the Cameroons, Niger, Burkina-Faso, Sudan, etc.; and the Water Company of Lyons in Senegal, etc.

8. The explanation we propose is drawn from a synthesis of different articles published in the press after the resignation of Jean-Pierre Cot. We have added information that we have received from groups of militants.

7. British Responsibilities in Africa

It is none too easy to present British policy in Africa. As far as we can see, it does not present the clear-cut outlines which characterize the policies of America, France or the USSR. The very difficulties we experienced in finding documents which refer to it go a long way to justify this intuition. There is no incisive strategy, but a course of action in conformity with British tradition: pragmatic, supple, in half-tones, and very often following the same goals as America.

It is a curious fact that when we asked for information on British 'policy', the answer always referred to British 'assistance', as if the nation which, in the 19th and 20th Centuries, had been the greatest colonial power, no longer had any political link or economic interests to defend overseas. Guilt, trickery, real detachment, or a little of all three? That is what we are going to try to spell out by examining the practical result of this position in some of Britain's former colonies where tragedies have ensued. Then we should be able to measure the responsibility to be attributed to Great Britain.

Generally speaking, we can agree with George Padmore[1] that when decolonization took place there was no single approach to the problem: in Eastern, Central and Southern Africa, Great Britain supports the settlers and European domination, whereas in West Africa, where Britain has never meant to favour settlements, the Colonial Office advocates the principle of self-determination with successive constitutional reforms. One thing is certain: the common enemy everywhere is communism, but the means taken to avoid it are very different. The British system offers the subject peoples many more opportunities to achieve self-determination than the French colonial system, which is more centralizing. Great Britain had never admitted representatives from the colonies to the British Parliament; each colony had its own Parliament and was encouraged to develop its own institutions, and this was to make the road to independence much easier.

Then what is behind the blunders in Kenya, Uganda, Zimbabwe and Southern Africa, to quote only these examples? The gap which separates the intention from the realization will be very harmful to the process of independence, and problems will arise wherever there are large numbers of White settlers. When the subject peoples do not force her hand, Great Britain will always give 'too little and too late', provoking resentment and even hatred among her subjects.

The Africans first protested against the slow progress made in their territories (Uganda and Kenya) and the fact that they were not treated on an equal basis with the Whites. This inequality between Blacks and Whites created bad feelings and encumbered what could have been an easy path towards independence.

Decolonization in Kenya: History Always Repeats Itself

At the end of the last century, in order to build the railway between Mombasa and Kampala for commercial and military reasons, it was necessary to cross the centre of the high table-land of Kenya, where the land belonged to the Kikuyu, Maasai and Wakambe tribes. To avoid attacks on the railway by the angry tribes, Sir Charles Eliot, then Governor of Kenya, decided to requisition the land for the White settlers. The tribes responded by occupying the land (squatting), and on top of it all they were taxed and impressed for forced labour.

The cruelty of the settlers favoured the revolt of the Mau Mau, as the British called them to cover them with discredit and justify the repression. This revolt was a spontaneous result of the dispossession of the tribes. The people were forced to settle in town slums and condemned to redundancy. In 1954, Nairobi already counted 10,000 young Blacks without work, hope or resources, some of whom could see no other solution to their problems than to engage in crime. They held the Whites responsible and fought to recover their land and their work. But their representation in Parliament was ridiculous: while 30,000 Whites returned fourteen members, 5,500,000 Kenyans had only six.

Instead of answering the claims of the Kenyans by taking social measures, the settlers put pressure on the administration to resist and pass measures of repression. The Kenyan African Union, a legal organization grouping the advocates of independence, came under these laws and Jomo Kenyatta, who was a member of this party, was among those arrested. The process of violence and war had begun, and what was at the outset simply a state of emergency developed into the most important colonial struggle since the Boer War. It is not difficult to imagine the effect on the Kikuyu and the emigrations that followed.

The British again resorted to the old trick: *'divide et impera'*. The government encouraged chieftains and puppets in their pay to form organizations apparently fighting for independence and so thwarted the united front. From the beginning the Secret Services helped to defeat the Land Freedom Army (LFA), fighting for the freedom of Kenya, and to install a neo-colonial system controlled by Britain. Frank Kitson, the best known of the Military Intelligence Officers (the MIO is a branch of the

61

Intelligence Service) was to recruit among his troops a certain Idi Amin Dada . . . These specialists, with the help of traitors from the ranks of the Land Freedom Army, spread terror among the population and provoked new flights. The resistance of the Mau Mau was crushed in 1960: now that the radical LFA movement had no leader Britain could safely grant independence. The moderate Jomo Kenyatta was triumphally elected the following year (1961).

In Uganda: Blunders against a Background of Tragedy

Milton Obote was far from being a progressive leader and he was no danger at all to British interests, but he was not well received by the western countries. His diplomatic policy, direct and non-aligned, and his preference for a global solution in Africa made him look like a supporter of the Soviets in East Africa where Tanzania was already sporting social-ist theories and where the Economic Community was not a success. So when Obote decided to nationalize 80 British firms, it was no surprise that the British expressed alarm. Taking advantage of the absence of Obote at the Commonwealth Conference in 1971, they used the Military Intellig-ence Service (MIS) and the Israeli Mossad to devise a plot to put Idi Amin Dada in power.

Amin Dada broke with the policy of Obote and relied on a local bourgeoisie associated with British economic interests. Unhappily for these people the colt broke free, dispensed with the leading citizens of the former regime and established a dictatorship, making fools of those who had sponsored him. Despite its riches, the country was bankrupt. There was nothing inventive about this corrupt regime, characterized by poverty and repression on one side, and by corruption, contraband and the search for profits on the other.

But as Washington showed rather too much interest in Idi Amin Dada, London continued to give him support. Convinced that if he were thrown out he would be replaced by a pro-communist regime, the British let him indulge in massacres which exceeded the limits of horror and caused the terror-stricken population to flee. Only when Amin Dada showed signs of friendship with Gadhafi did London decide to act. Territorial claims on Tanzania provided a pretext. The Secret Services gave their support to the intervention of Tanzanian troops in Uganda.

After ten years of this cruel regime, Uganda was ruined and a starving population was already on the roads, when a drought swept through the country and pushed back the limits of despair. The international com-munity could not afford to leave such a zone of insecurity between Zaire, Ethiopia and South Africa, and the level of international aid rose to match the extent of their fears. But no such assistance can save a country if the traditional social relations of the neo-colonial system are not ended. And in the Tanzanian army which invaded Uganda there were not only thousands of refugees, but also the politicians removed by Amin Dada and a horde of civil servants belonging to the lower middle classes. The small tradesmen covered the country like a wave, full of a new hope, intent on power and profit.

After the elections of May 1981, Yusuf Lule and Lugongwa Binaisa were quickly replaced at the head of the country by a military junta. Famine was rife in the countryside, but in the towns the middle classes were making money. On the international level, Western imperialism dictated its policy with the threat of food shortage, and national and international agencies competed to provide assistance (Oxfam, US Care, Comité Catholique, Red Cross, EEC, the UN . . .). The lorries which carried this food were attacked and pillaged. The distress of a country manipulated by foreign interests and the greed of its local bourgeoisie was pitiful to see, but this was the only way imperialism could re-establish order and avoid a regime too closely linked to Tanzanian 'socialism'.

Rhodesia-Zimbabwe: Snatching Victory from Defeat

The story of Zimbabwe is simply that of Kenya in a more tragic form. Rhodesia was peopled by a large white minority, whose special status was due to its history and close economic links with the mother country. This explains why the colony did not obtain independence at the same time as the others.

But in May 1965 the disagreement between the White settlers and the Labour government on one hand and the practical co-ordination reached between the Black freedom movements[2] on the other, led the government of Ian Smith to proclaim unilaterally the independence of Rhodesia. Great Britain refused to recognize this and continued to consider Rhodesia as a British colony, while the country became a huge prison for the Africans, who seemed to expect that their freedom would come from Great Britain.

Harold Wilson, who was then in power, enacted a series of economic, financial and juridical means of retaliation against the Smith government, but London showed little determination, faced with strong reprisals from Salisbury. In May 1968 the UN, under pressure from the OAU, decided on a complete embargo, but Great Britain kept up the contacts. Wilson met Smith on the HMS *Fearless*, and later on HMS *Tiger*. In 1971 a compromise was reached under which the Africans were the real losers: London recognized the Rhodesian constitution of 1969, which imposed clearly the domination of the Whites. As a red herring, Ian Smith tried to put forward Bishop Muzorewa, a moderate individual totally devoted to the interests of the White community. This compromise needed to be ratified by all the people living in the country, Blacks and Whites together. The Pearce Commission was sent out to investigate on the spot the feelings of the Africans, but an upsurge in favour of rejection swept through the country like a forest fire. This refusal meant losing the economic advantages offered by Great Britain and intensifying a dignified struggle for independence despite the destitution that this implied and the hunger and exile that accompanied it.

In the spring of 1979 the Conservatives came to power. Mrs Thatcher had never hidden her preference for Muzorewa, and she turned her back on the solutions proposed by Andrew Young, the American representative at the UN, and David Owen, the former Labour Minister for Foreign Affairs. The Conservative plan sought: (1) to put aside the Liberation Front; (2) to recognize Muzorewa and establish a situation similar to that in Kenya, while assuring a rearguard for the Western powers in South Africa; (3) to count on the lassitude and the economic exhaustion of the neighbouring states (Zambia, Mozambique and Tanzania) to isolate the fighters of the Zimbabwe African National Liberation Army (ZANLA). On the other hand, the trap which the Labour government had set for Ian Smith's government was far from watertight. Firms had gone on trading with Rhodesia, and the pro-Rhodesian lobby in London found no difficulty in protecting its economic interests more openly.

The Black people's fight for freedom was to be punctuated by military, ideological and political successes, by secessions from unity, by poverty and by flights, but also by various conferences: at Victoria Falls in 1975, at Geneva in 1976, and at Malta in 1976 and 1977. Finally Lord Soames, named governor for the transition period, arrived at Salisbury on 12 December 1979. The revolt of the White settlers was hushed up and during the transition period Rhodesia again became a British colony. The Conference of Lancaster House offered the ravaged colony political independence, while mooring it firmly in the waters of western imperialism.

The most important section of the agreement concerned the land, for which the Africans had fought so hard. Land was to be sold, not distributed, and the indemnification made easier by the British government, which agreed to pay half the price of the redistribution. Mugabe returned in triumph, but if he and his people had chosen to refuse the deal and choose the way of socialism, the result would have been the exodus of the Whites and loss of their expertise. The country would have been in the same situation as Angola and Mozambique in 1975, undermined by the efforts of South Africa to provoke unrest. The same applied to the industrial sector, where 70% of the holdings were in the hands of transnationals. The Anglo-American transnationals based in South Africa own nearly all the sugar industry, the mines and the building firms, and have important holdings in the banks and financial companies. They are powerful enough to be able to pursue an unrestrained economic policy in their own interests, and with no thought for the interests of Zimbabwe.

These facts partly explain the frustration of the people, be they freedom fighters or not, who had put all their hope in the restitution of the land and recovering the mastery of the national economy. The lack of work and the unchanged labour relations fed the disenchantment of those who were soon to break away. It is important not to confound these dissidents with the counter-revolutionaries who were armed by South Africa and based on her territory. But the fact remains that the revolt which rumbles in Matabeleland is playing the game of South Africa, who keeps it going. In the meantime, 165 officers of the British army are training the army of Zimbabwe, which perpetrates the massacres in Matabeleland and forces the populations they threaten to join the flow of refugees.

This is the way British imperialism, fully conscious of its economic interests, has succeeded in taking over the military victory won by ZANU-ZAPU, while at the same time preventing outbreaks of revolt like that of the OAS,[3] which Ian Smith and his supporters had hoped for. The Lancaster House agreements gave substantial guarantees to private capital, almost entirely from Anglo-Saxon sources, but also paved the way for a rebellion.

Namibia Still under the Rod of South Africa

The role of Great Britain in Namibia is determined by its economic interests in the region. Namibia is the only country in Africa still under foreign domination. It was entrusted to South Africa after 1918, and should have acquired national sovereignty at the end of the Second World War, had not South Africa continued to ignore resolution no. 435 of the UN in favour of its independence. Its eventual accession to independence has been entrusted to a Contact Group comprising the United States, Canada, West Germany, France and Great Britain.

Under the Labour government, David Owen, helped by Andrew Young, the American representative at the UN, played an important part in trying to put South Africa outside international law. This did not, however, stop Great Britain from honouring her illegal contracts to buy uranium from the Rössing mine, the first uranium mine in the world, where the British firm Rio Tinto Zinc holds the major stake. The principal contracts with Rössing were signed at the Ministry of Energy by the Labour minister Anthony Wedgwood Benn. Rio Tinto Zinc obtained a new source of profit and strengthened its position on the world market, while Great Britain procured the energy necessary for her nuclear programme at a reasonable price.

There was no danger that the situation would change when the Conservatives followed the Labour Party, especially as the new Head of the Foreign Office, Lord Carrington, was a former director of Rio Tinto Zinc. Together with France, West Germany, Switzerland, Holland, Japan and the USSR, Great Britain went on buying uranium oxide from Rössing, and pillaging the other mines in Namibia, while voicing her doubts as to the impartiality of the Contact Group with regard to the South West African People's Organization (SWAPO).

Finally South Africa agreed to sit at the Geneva Conference in January 1981 to negotiate a plan of disengagement. Despite the moderate attitude of SWAPO, and her own desire to sign a cease-fire and to safeguard the recognition of the UN, South Africa capsized the conference without giving the slightest sign of good will. This categorical attitude could have been an indication that Botha, the South African Prime Minister, needed to strengthen his position before the elections, and that he had no clear idea how to get out of Namibia without setting a tidal wave in motion in favour of SWAPO. But he also knew that he was supported by the British government which, with the help of Reagan, opened up new possibilities to manoeuvre in the Contact Group.

What is certain is that, at the end of the negotiations, West Germany, France and Canada took a tougher stand against the RSA, whereas Reagan and Mrs Thatcher tried to draw her into the western camp. The USA deplored the system of apartheid in their speeches, but considered South Africa as the best bulwark against communism. The question to be discussed was whether South Africa should fight communism on the border between Namibia and Angola, or on that which separates Namibia from South Africa, it being well understood that the withdrawal of South African troops from Namibia was linked with the withdrawal of Cuban soldiers from Angola. Under pressure from Great Britain and the United States, the Contact Group was in complete dissension. It was Claude Cheysson, the new Minister for Foreign Affairs of the left-wing government in France, who obliged the Anglo-Americans to beat a provisional retreat, and Great Britain was alone with the US in using her veto on the vote of sanctions against the RSA.

As to what concerns the refugees, the systematic bombardment of Angola by South African troops, with the covert support of Great Britain, was a continuing cause of the flight from home of the harassed population.

British Pragmatism

These are a few examples to illustrate British policy in Africa. It is not a clearly defined strategy, as is that of France. Rather more a flexible attitude, inherited from her colonial policy and now reflecting or reacting against the policy of America.

For example, Great Britain did not respond to the American system of imperial relays, as did Giscard d'Estaing.[4] But that did not prevent Britain from being openly present on the economic level, controlling the mines and investing via the intermediary of its transnational corporations. Unilever puts 12% of its capital in the United African Corporation (UAC) and announces cynically: 'We invest money where we hope to make money.' UAC also invests in Ghana: in cars, in mineral water, in beer and in cement-works, in agreement with Portland Cement . . . In order to guarantee her exchange reserves and reinforce her prestige among the banks and the position of the London money market, Great Britain has always tried to keep her former colonies in the Sterling Area, in the same way as France has acted with regard to the Franc zone.

The past and present collusion of Great Britain with the worst kind of regimes is always determined by her economic interests: there is nothing very unusual in that! In South Africa, the economic and military interests of the United States have carried off the first place, but Great Britain remains the second commercial partner and the first investor in this country. Despite the official statements which deny that any deals have taken place, the Conservative government is still selling military material and gave Mr Botha a long hearing when he visited Europe in June 1984.

More subtle and sagacious than France under Giscard, Great Britain had a more guarded attitude towards the role of the west in the affair of Shaba. But David Owen himself has said that the examples of Entebbe and Kolwezi enabled him to see the possibility of military intervention in Rhodesia in a different light. Be she governed by a Labour or a Conservative government, Great Britain acts always more or less as the shadow of the US. It is tempting to make use of the image employed by George Padmore[5] to define the relations between states in the Commonwealth: 'as separate as the fingers of the hand when the interests of each country are at stake, but united as the fist' in all points touching the interests of western capitalism.

Despite the dramatic examples of opportunities that have been lost, and the obstinacy and shortsightedness of the White minorities, British policy is the reflection of her colonial policy. During the years of colonization, the British built up, by rule of thumb, a flexible and adaptable system which naturally allowed them to disengage less abruptly than other colonial powers, like France, and generally more completely. We can only regret that, here as elsewhere, the pressure of the settlers and economic interests still in place have been the cause of tragic sideslips which have engendered, among other consequences, new streams of refugees in this suffering land of Africa.

Notes

1. George Padmore, *Panafricanism or Communism? The Coming Struggle for Africa* (London, Dennis Dobson, 1959). Cf. p. 200 in the French translation.

2. The Zimbabwe African National Union (ZANU) and the Zimbabwe African People's Union (ZAPU).

3. The Organization of the Secret Army (OAS) became infamous for its crimes and tortures during the war between Algeria and France. It was inspired by an ideology of the extreme right.

4. President of France from 1974 to 1981. See Chapter 6.

5. George Padmore, *Panafricanism or Communism?* (French translation), p. 204.

8. Causes and Responsibilities to be Found Throughout Africa

Apparently the wave of refugees in Africa was closely linked with the claim of most African countries to self-determination, and it could be thought that after independence it would have stopped, or at least slowed down. Unhappily this did not prove to be the case, and the number of refugees, which was about 200,000 in 1950, was multiplied by five during the 1960s, which are generally considered to be the years of African independence. Today there are between 5 million and 6 million people considered as refugees in Africa.

It is true that independence was often fictitious, but the permanence or even the resurgence of the refugee problem after it was achieved has obliged us to look for other causes and responsibilities. In the course of this research we have tried:
— to identify the conflicts and tensions peculiar to African countries which have aggravated the refugee problem;
— to discover other conflicts and tensions which originate in the relations between the African states;
— to go more deeply into the role of the OAU, as its contradictions play an integral part in these conflicts and tensions.

The after effects of decolonization, especially when this was improvized by the colonial power, had of course a part in creating these tensions, and in some cases even caused the emigration of whole classes of the population. But there are other causes, which have their origin in African traditions or mentalities, or in the very inexperience of the new African states. Among these we can mention:

● the absence of democracy;
● the lack of religious tolerance;
● the rivalries between peoples, tribes and clans;
● and the lack of stability of the new political regimes.

The After Effects of Decolonization

A careful examination of the relations entertained by the colonial powers with their 'subjects' in different countries allows us to affirm that there were practically two kinds of 'subjects': those who were privileged to be the intermediaries between the colonial masters and the people they had colonized (we could call them the relays of the colonial power in the country) and the rest of the population. It was easier and more efficacious for the colonial power to depend on a tribe or a group of tribes which had the reputation of being powerful or well organized.

This strategy was regularly used in the case of indirect colonization, and a little less frequently where colonization was direct. Where colonization and its administration was indirect, the colonial power could easily attribute its own failures to the administrative relay. When the rest of the population contested the relay, the colonial authority could cease to back it. It could even take arms against the former relay if the situation demanded it. The case of Rwanda is a good example of this.

Without going into all the details of a long and complex history of decolonization, Rwanda, and her southern neighbour, Burundi, were former German possessions. Considered as territories under mandate in the context of the League of Nations, they were entrusted to Belgium under the regular control of the UN. Belgium could not use the same methods of administration she used in the Congo, which was her own colony. That is why she upheld the indigenous institutions to establish her authority. But these institutions were under the unique control of the Tutsi, in a country where the Hutu and the Twa also dwelt and even formed the majority of the population.

According to Robert Cornevin,[1] it is difficult to fix the date when the Tutsi entered the region. He believes that they came from the north-east of Africa, from the countries of Ndorwa and Mpororo. According to this source, there were many marriages between the Tutsi aristocracy (of whom there were a limited number) and Hutu women. Such a reading of history is not shared by the great majority of the Tutsi, as it portrays them as strangers in their own country. In any case, this was the theme exploited by the leaders of the Hutu for the first time about 1959, the year when the first wave of refugees fled from Rwanda to the neighbouring countries, as we shall see below.

Several authors, however, recognize that the Tutsi were most of them well-exercised fighters who had no other occupation but to look after their herds, while the Hutu were occupied almost entirely with the cultivation of the lands: war held no interest for them, except, of course, if they were attacked. The defence of the territory was thus left to the Tutsi. As for the Twa or Tvides, considered as the pygmies of the land, they had no interest in defence, nor even in tilling the fields, as their way of life was extremely simple (hunting and fruit-picking).

German colonization, followed by the administration of Belgium, maintained in Rwanda, as in Burundi, the traditional political structures, entirely controlled by the Tutsi. Belgian colonization opened the schools to the Tutsi, but not to the Hutu. The few Hutus who received instruction came from the Seminaries.[2] They were almost entirely absent from the administration, as the Belgians recruited their collaborators among the Tutsi and the Congolese. In the police force and the colonial army, no citizen from Rwanda (be he Tutsi, Hutu or Twa) was admitted: only Congolese were allowed to follow a military career in Rwanda as in Burundi.

But when the wind of independence swept over Africa, cries were heard in Rwanda, as elsewhere. The tragic death of Mwami Mtara V, in rather equivocal circumstances, was the beginning of tension between the Tutsi and the Belgian colonial administration.[3] This tension was at first local, but it was later generalized, and the creation by the Tutsi of the National Rwandese Union (UNAR), a political revolutionary movement aiming at the immediate and complete independence of Rwanda, made the dispute with Belgium even more serious.

The Tutsi minority had now become a burden for the Belgians. They tried to isolate them by encouraging the Hutu to oppose the UNAR. A moderate independence party was established for the Hutu (under the name of Permuhutu) which easily won the elections organized by the colonial administration.

It is understandable that the Tutsi were unable to accept this defeat, as they did not consider the elections democratic. On the other hand, the Hutu were unable to master the elation they felt as a result of the 'victory', and a considerable tension resulted which degenerated into armed confrontation between the Tutsi and the Hutu. It all sprang from what was, all told, an unimportant incident: some young Tutsi had provoked a minor Hutu chieftain. The chieftain reacted violently, and the Hutu retaliated by attacking the village of Nidza, where a Tutsi chieftain had his residence. Tutsi reprisals followed immediately, out of all proportion to the incident, which is easy to understand as they were professional warriors. The evidence gathered by an international expert[4] shows that they formed groups or commandos directed against the Hutu with appalling results: 'plunder, the burning of huts, murders, aggressions, etc.'

This was the moment chosen by the colonial administration to intervene — on the side of the Hutu, of course. The Tutsi leaders were pursued and arrested, or put under house arrest, until the elections of 25 September 1961. Under these conditions the Hutu were sure to win the elections at the expense of the Tutsi.

Held at bay in this way, the Tutsi stepped up their action against the colonial administration. This was styled 'subversive activity' so that its authors could be pursued and repressed. And, indeed, their outbursts were not simply aimed against their political adversaries, the Hutu, but against all signs of Belgian colonization in the country. The colonial administration answered by launching abhorrent massacres of the Tutsi and provoking their flight into exile towards Uganda and what is now Zaire. When Burundi, Tanganyika and Kenya in their turn received independence, a second, more numerous, wave of Tutsi refugees sought a home in these countries, where they are still living. According to the UN HCR, there are about 200,000 Rwandese refugees in Burundi, 40,000 in Tanzania and 2,000 in Kenya. Almost all of them were obliged to leave Rwanda because of conflicts and tensions which were peculiar to the country, but in which the colonial administration has a responsibility because of their failure to decolonize successfully.

The case of the refugees from Sudan is now settled, but it is worth examining, as it is a clear example of the responsibility of a former colonial power in the conflicts and tensions peculiar to African countries. Of course, as in many other cases, it would be incorrect to reduce to this single factor the causes of the tensions which engender the refugee movement. The global analysis of many cases shows that the conflicts and tensions are so interconnected that no single factor can explain what happened. But having made allowance for this fact, the colonial responsibility seems to have been particularly determining in the events of Sudan, even in the civil wars, as well as in those of Rwanda. In order to understand the events which shook Sudan, and especially the southern part of the country, and led to streams of refugees leaving the country, we studied the following factors:

1) British colonization had imposed a different evolution in the north and south of the country. The obvious reasons are strategical, but the following command the attention:

● *the absence of geographical unity:* the north is situated in a zone of savanna grasslands and sub-arid steppes, whereas the south is a mosaic of sub-equatorial and tropical forests;

● *the absence of tribal unity:* in this part of Africa Sudan is the hinge between the Arab and the Black populations, but the cross-breeding between the two races, which has been going on now for centuries, has been unable to do away with the typically Arab tribes in the north and the typically Black tribes in the south.

2) Among the historical causes, we can point out:

● *the Arab incursions to capture Black slaves,* without forgetting the savage nature of the Mahdist movement[5] against the populations of the south.

● *the Anglo-Egyptian tutelage.*[6]

● *unequal access to education* in the north (with 7,000 pupils in 1955) and in the south (25,000 pupils at the same date). This will result in the Christians of the south becoming the pick of the population, and they are disinclined to Islam. In the north, Arabic is the common language, whereas in the south the colonial masters have cultivated the myth of the language of Shakespeare. In the mid-1950s Great Britain changed her strategy and united the two sections of the country, which had up to then been

71

administered separately, the pretext being that Egypt was about to claim the northern part of Sudan. The origin of the conflict between the north and the south is here: the north would prefer the country to remain undivided, while the south desires a federation, which would leave them independent of the north.

3) Then there are economic reasons:

We have already said that the north is a barren zone, and this implies that most of Sudan's riches are to be found in the south. A major mistake was made when negotiating the decolonization: the Cairo Agreements[7] were negotiated without any representative from the south, and the decolonization was realized at the expense of the southern province. To have refused these warring brothers a legal debate in democratic conditions was to lay the basis for tensions which were to develop into armed conflict and finally, as we shall see, into civil war.

Rwanda and Sudan have shown how deep can be the after effects of decolonization in Africa. We have concluded that the mother countries contrived to establish strategic situations which were to allow them to develop conflicts, or to sow the germs of hidden tensions, in order to manipulate one or the other of the elements of the population in accordance with their current interests.

The Absence of Democracy

At a time when most of the African countries were engaged in a struggle for freedom it was easy to understand the stream of refugees, but it is paradoxical to remark that, instead of disappearing, this phenomenon has taken on serious proportions. We are obliged to affirm that the influence of the former colonial powers, even if still visible in certain domains, cannot be denounced as the only factor responsible for the lack of democratic institutions in the new states. Speaking generally, this rejection of democracy is to be found: in the rejection of alternation in the government; in ideological intolerance; in the numerous military dictatorships.

Where they refuse to accept alternation in the exercise of power, the African countries justify this by claiming that they are young countries, in need of institutional stability, which is in their eyes a guarantee of the economic development of their country. They achieve their ends by any means to hand:

● by constantly adapting their constitutions to fit the situation, or only applying them when they can be used against personal or political adversaries;

● by regularly gerrymandering the elections: the 'father of the nation', 'the supreme guide', enlightened or enlightening, depending on whether he receives the light or is himself the light, disguises his intention to stay at the head of the country for life but always, in order to appear trustworthy, makes an excellent score at the elections — 99.99% of the votes expressed, for example!

● by imposing on the country a single party: an oligarchy, or even a single individual, dictates his ideas to the population as a whole, false as they may be!

● by establishing the cult of a personality, in order to give his authority a more solid base. This is the reign of marshals, of presidents for life, of emperors . . .

Naturally, established in these conditions, these powers accept no ideological differences. Every suspected opponent is hunted down.

Naturally this state of things is not the prerogative of any one type of state in Africa. Nearly all the African countries are concerned, whether they carry the label 'liberal' or proclaim that they are 'progressive'. And that is why it is to be feared that the stream of refugees will remain a permanent fact, even after the fictive independence of the African states. For the arbitrary rule of injustice and terror will not put an end to the emigration of whole peoples.

What we find peculiar to Africa is the fact that arbitrary rule, injustice and terror are not only directed against those who are supposedly the authors of 'political infractions'; they also affect their families, their friends and more distant relations, the members of their tribes. It is easy to understand that in such an atmosphere whole families and even villages leave the country: men, women and children, young folk and even old people are on the run, with their livestock. Guinea, Zaire, Angola and Uganda are illustrations of the fact that the movement of refugees has continued in Africa, and has even become generalized.

Since 1958, the date of its independence, to 1984, Guinea only had one party, the Democratic Party of Guinea (PDG), and one president, Mr Sekou Touré. Every attempt, well-founded or rash, to overthrow this government was severely repressed. In these conditions it is not surprising that in a short time the refugees from this country numbered more than a million: all the neighbouring countries are invaded by them and the international organizations are overwhelmed.

Zaire is a country in which the word democracy has no meaning. Since he took power in 1965, Mr Mobutu has done all he can to eliminate his opponents, direct or indirect. He started by gerrymandering the elections, and has ended by nominating people chosen in the party which he has founded and of which he remains president for life. Every attempt to oppose him, from within the country or from without, has been put down with bloodshed. Members of Parliament who resist are arrested, tortured and humiliated. A security police has been organized and reinforced: they use more and more sophisticated means of torture. The people are muzzled: every individual liberty is suppressed, and political assassinations are carefully organized (disappearances, car accidents, poisonings . . .). Special services exist to track down suspects . . . 'Whether you will or not', it is to be read in Article 7 of the Zairese Constitution, 'you are a member of the Popular Movement of the Revolution (MRP).' Counter-revolutionaries, be they imperialists or 'subversive elements' working for Moscow, are all destined to the same fate. The situation in such a country can only invite its inhabitants to resort to exile.

Angola brings further evidence. This country became independent after a long and deadly fight for freedom, but was not to find peace after its freedom has been won. For the Popular Movement for the Liberation of Angola (MPLA) took power alone, to the detriment of the two other components of the armies of liberation, the National Front for the Liberation of Angola (FNLA) and the National Union for the Total Liberation of Angola (UNITA). These two movements have regrouped their members on the road to exile, and some have moved underground. More than 500,000 people have returned as refugees to Zaire and Zambia, where they have already spent several years of their lives.

In Uganda, the accession to power of General Idi Amin Dada, and above all the way he ran the country, obliged men, women and children to flee to Zaire, Kenya or Tanzania. The return of the former President Obote resulted in a massive return of these Ugandan refugees, but new emigrations were to take place towards Rwanda, Kenya and Tanzania . . . In this ebb and flow of Ugandan refugees, those who have suffered most are those who speak Kinyarwanda.[8] They are natives of Rwanda and have settled in south-west Uganda in three distinct stages during the past 70 years.

At the end of the First World War the Belgians, masters of Rwanda at the time, transferred to Great Britain, the master of Uganda, part of the north-west of Rwanda. The people living in this part of Rwanda became Ugandan. Between the two wars, Rwanda was over-populated and became a reserve of labour for the Belgian Congo, Tanganyika and Uganda. That is why today it is still possible to find Rwandese populations living in Zaire, quite a distance from the sub-region of Kivu, mainly around the mining zones (for example in the Shaba, formerly known as Katanga). A third wave of refugees was caused by the Rwandese civil war at the time of independence. As we have said, only people belonging to this group have the strict right to be called 'refugees'. Their number is estimated at 80,000. It is surprising to state that there is now a question of 500,000 persons being expelled by Uganda under the pretext that they are refugees on her territory and natives of Rwanda.

But when they try to re-enter Rwanda, only 6,000 of these people have been accepted by the authorities as inhabitants of the country, and all of these are Hutu! The figure seems ridiculous, but all the other people are considered by Rwanda as refugees. It seems aberrant to be called a refugee in one's own country!

Religious Intolerance

The new African leaders are incapable of respecting the rules of democracy, and this applies also to the field of religion. Hardly surprising, when we realize that democracy is non-existent. In these republics, only the religion professed by the chief tells the truth. Hesitant subjects are sometimes 'converted' by force, and those who resist are persecuted if they do not choose exile. We have already explained how that happened in Sudan; it also happened in Chad.

In this country, the French colonizers, unable to introduce Christianity in the Moslem north, turned to the south of the country, created schools and opened the way to modern knowledge to the Black populations of this region. The majority of the people working for the colonial administration came from this part of the country, and when Chad acceded to independence, power was entrusted to François Tombalbaye, a former school-teacher from the south. The populations of the north contested his authority, and created an opposition movement to voice their claims, the National Liberation Front of the Chad (FROLINAT). Taking refuge in the neighbouring countries (the Niger, Libya and Algeria), the soldiers of Frolinat harassed the government of Tombalbaye and provoked his fall. This was undoubtedly made easier by the coup d'état brought about by General Felix Malloum who, like Tombalbaye, came from the south. The failure of his movement can be attributed in part to his southern origins, although other problems contributed. He found himself unable to restore the unity of the country and to assure a minimum of economic and social development after the disastrous administration of the preceding regime. But his principal failure was his inability to put down the rebellion which had long been smouldering in the north. Numerous battles took place between the troops faithful to the government and those of the Frolinat, and heavy losses of life and material were suffered by both sides. This conflict has obliged and still obliges thousands of people to leave their homes and seek shelter. They prefer to seek refuge in neighbouring countries, inside the borders of which neither the government's troops nor those supporting the rebellion can venture.

These different conflicts and tensions between people living in Chad are an important source of refugees for the countries in the region. They often result from the cultural differences between the north and the south, exacerbated by the influence of Islam, Christianity and Animism. For the north of the Chad belongs to the vast Islamic culture, whereas the south, which is Christian or Animist, has already been opened up to other cultures, for the historical reasons we have already cited when discussing Sudan (raids, the slave trade . . .).

Racial, Tribal or Individual Rivalries

While examining the conflicts and tensions provoked by or originating from the after effects of colonialism (Sudan) or religious intolerance (Chad), we have been confronted with racial problems. This approach to the question can be applied to all African countries whose population is composed of numerous socio-cultural groups (different religions, races or tribes). We can apply it to Mauretania, Nigeria, the Niger, Ethiopia, Somalia, Zaire, etc. It can also be extended to the countries peopled by large tribes which belong to different religions, as in Nigeria. We shall come back to this case. But we should note that, as in countries with different races, the race or group of races in power take advantage of their position to crush the others. They exercise their domination politically, economically, culturally, and even, as we have just seen, religiously. And if by chance the underdogs try to lift up their heads, the use of the national army will re-establish order, be it at the cost of bloodshed.

The populations against whom these measures are directed will evidently seek refuge without waiting for the arrival of the government's troops. They may go to their native province, and work henceforward for its self-determination, or more often, to foreign countries in the neighbourhood. Nigeria seems a good case to illustrate this aspect of the question, although a solution has now been found.

British colonial rule in Nigeria was a typical example of indirect administration. This reinforced the cultural and economic differences between the Hausa and the Igbos and at the hour of independence left the greater part of the power in the hands of the Hausa who tried to impose their authority on the other tribes. But the Igbos, who were in a majority in the educated classes of the country, were not prepared to leave the hegemony to the Hausa. They created their own state, Biafra, distinct from Nigeria. The strong reaction of the central power against this rebellious province caused the Igbo population to seek refuge outside the country.

In this case, as in so many others, tribal rivalries, often forgotten by the populations concerned, have been awakened by those in power or by outside factors, and have become important causes of the continuing stream of refugees in Africa. But these rivalries are not merely racial or tribal, they are also clannish and even individual. It is quite common to see two clans fighting, not for the good of the country or even the interests of the men in power, but simply for objectives which interest the clans. The struggle for power takes place in the same socio-cultural group.

But the most intensive rivalries are those which oppose individuals to the other members of the socio-cultural group because of their quest for personal satisfaction. This may simply create tensions, but it often leads to murderous conflicts as recently in the Chad. Goukouni and Habré were both members of the Frolinat fighting against the regime of Tombalbaye, but they then formed two sub-groups in this organization and caused the troubles which we have just been discussing. It is true that the two men hold different views: one is progressive, the other moderate, but it is above all a battle between two personalities who detest one another heartily. And the most regrettable aspect of this situation is that the populations of Chad are running in every direction to find peace in the neighbouring states.

The Instability of the Political Regimes

Sudden changes in the political regimes, for example because of frequent cruel coups d'état, inevitably help to destabilize the populations. This has proved true in Uganda, Central Africa, Benin (at that time called Dahomey), and more recently still in Burkina-Faso (then still known as Upper Volta).

Such are the principal causes and responsibilities of the African states themselves in the eternal problem of the refugees in Africa.

Notes

1. Robert Cornevin, *Histoire des Peuples de l'Afrique Noire*, édit. Payot (Petite Collection Payot, Paris, 1959), pp. 554–5.

2. Establishments of secondary or superior grade teaching destined to form future indigenous priests.

3. The Mwami was the sovereign of Rwanda. The colonial administration had reduced his importance to that of a Big Chief under the King of the Belgians. Unverified rumours would have it that this sovereign was put to death by the Belgian colonial administration, which had never forgiven him for having tried to renew his relations with West Germany.

4. These details were communicated by Mr Baillot, engineer and international expert in agronomy, at the Conference of the Centre of Advanced Studies on Africa and Asia Minor (CHEAM), which was held at the University of Paris, under the direction of Professor Froelich.

5. In some Moslem sects the name of Mahdi is given to an Envoy of Allah, who is expected to fulfil the work of Mahomet. In the context, the name designates a former sultan of Sudan who, in the 19th Century, claimed to be the Mahdi. A hardy warrior, he revolted against the Egyptians and resisted British colonialism for a long time.

6. Sudan became an Anglo-Egyptian condominium in 1935.

7. The Cairo Agreements allowed Great Britain to define the different stages through which Sudan must pass before reaching her independence in 1956.

8. Kinyarwanda is the language spoken in Rwanda by the autochthonous populations.

9. Tensions and Conflicts Between African States

It is true that a number of the tensions and conflicts which generate the movement of refugees come from the very nature of African states, but there are others, just as important, which are rooted in the relations which these states maintain with one another. The creation of the Organization of African Unity (OAU) in 1963 was a reply to this problem, as we shall show. And that is the meaning of a number of principles inscribed in the Charter of this organization by the African states which created it.[1]

The following should be noted, as they touch the relations of those states which are members:

- the African states are rigorously equal one to the other;
- any effort to create subversion is forbidden;
- the borders of African states cannot be changed;
- African differences must be settled in Africa and by African organizations;
- the regions of Africa enjoy the right to pluralism.

Lack of respect towards one of these five principles does not necessarily lead to an open conflict between the states concerned, but it obviously creates tensions which are harmful to the peaceful development of Africa and cause the depopulation of many areas.

The tensions and conflicts which have broken the peace and contributed to the existence of refugees, directly or indirectly, seem mainly to have sprung from the failure to observe these principles of the Charter of the OAU:

- African borders cannot be changed;
- any effort to create subversion is forbidden;
- African differences must be settled in Africa by African organizations.[2]

Tensions and Conflicts along the Borders

Tensions and conflicts which spring from the failure to respect the intangibility of the frontiers seem to underline the importance given to this principle in Africa. We think immediately of the war which has been raging for several years between the countries of the Ogaden, especially Ethiopia and Somalia. Another important frontier conflict is that which opposes Libya and Chad, for the possession of the strip of land known as the Aouzou.

To these conflicts we can add that between Morocco and Mauretania, in which more than the question of frontiers is involved. Indeed Morocco questions the very existence of Mauretania as a state, and finds herself opposed today to the claims of the Sahraoui Republic by virtue of the same logic. The Sahraoui Republic is a country formed from the former Spanish possession called Rio de Oro or Western Sahara, but for Morocco it is simply a province of Morocco which was a victim of colonial divisions and which must be recovered. The Sahraoui people, supported by other neighbouring states, feel that their country should become a sovereign state. The size of this conflict and the time it has been going on continuously have provoked the emigration of the Sahraoui populations towards the neighbouring countries, especially to Algeria and Mauretania.

It may be useful to mention that tensions exist on numerous borders which the states concerned do not dare to recognize as such. These are called 'subversions', and attributed to the intrigues of the next-door neighbour.

Tensions and 'Subversions' Kept Alive from Abroad

When Zairese patriots, living in Angola, try to overthrow the government in power in Kinshasa, we imagine that the Russians and the Cubans are behind them. If an African leader denounces the exploitation of his country and of Africa as a whole, we only see his remarks as subversive . . . Should we not ask: What kind of subversion is it? The question is important, as it should be asked by all the African leaders rejected by their peoples. They feel that the subversion comes from their own citizens who have taken refuge abroad.

That is what was behind the meeting held in Zambia at the beginning of 1983 between Mobutu, Kaunda and Dos Santos.[3] It seems that some Zairese refugees in Zambia had taken part in a plot against Mr Kaunda, the president of Zambia. All these leaders have citizens who oppose their leadership on both sides of their frontiers, so they used the pretext of the plot in Zambia to decide to expel from their countries the 'subversive elements' from the other states. Angola and Zambia house Zairese refugees, Angola and Zaire have Zambian refugees, and in Zambia and Zaire there are refugees from Angola. These plans made it appear as if the different texts on refugees which had received international recognition (the Convention of the OAU and the Convention of Geneva signed in 1951) had become dead letters.

The major defect of the present frontiers is that they ignore tribal entities and even racial groups. They pass through these groups, but this can be an advantage for the exiles, as they do not feel so lost when they cross the borders of their country.

The Function of the OAU and its Contradictions

Soon after obtaining their independence, most African countries had to face the problem of refugees, most of whom came from countries which were not as yet independent. The new states assembled in a Pan-African organization and reached an agreement which enlarged the definition of a refugee. They agreed that:

> the term 'refugee' is to be applied to any person who, because of an aggression, of occupation by a foreign power, of foreign domination or of an event which seriously troubles public order in his region or in the whole of his country or the country of which he is a citizen, feels obliged to leave his usual residence to seek refuge somewhere outside his native country or the country of which he is a citizen.[4]

In accepting this definition, the countries which signed the agreement do not seem to have looked beyond the struggle they were waging against colonialism. Every African whose country, still under the colonial yoke, was invaded or at war against a colonial power, fell automatically into the category 'refugee'.

But now that the majority of African states have acquired their independence, refugees can no longer automatically benefit from the advantages defined in this agreement. Being a refugee in Africa no longer guarantees that the different texts about refugees will apply. You had hoped to find in a neighbouring country the opportunity to resist an arbitrary and bloodthirsty regime, but this is no longer the case. Today all that they can grant you is the right of political asylum, and even that is not assured: for if your own country demands your extradition, it will receive all the help it needs to recover you as soon as possible. So more and more Africans, faced with this insecurity, try to take refuge on other continents, especially in Europe.

One of the serious consequences of this emigration is that Africa is losing its brains and its energy. For in this exodus towards Europe are to be found the pick of the African populations, and also their youth. They are not only escaping from the uncompromising nature of African governments, but also from the economic, social and administrative disorder which accompanies them.

The number of refugees in Africa is increasing in a disturbing manner.

Colonization, neo-colonialism and all forms of imperialism are certainly at the root of this, but the African states also have a heavy responsibility by their very nature and the conception their rulers have of power. Despite the important influence of some of the historical and geographical factors that we have described, the permanence and the renewal of the phenomenon seems to depend more than anything else on politics.

For 'in African politics there is only the choice between three evils: absolute power, violent death and dishonourable exile'.[5] Absolute power allows no opposition and has the cult of unanimity, an ideal which it is difficult to realize. The practice of democratic debate was not frequent in pre-colonial Africa, nor anywhere else in the world for that matter. The absence of such a debate may be considered as one of the main causes of the problem of refugees in Africa today, for in every society there will always be some people who disagree with the political orientations taken and, unable to express their opinions, prefer to go into exile.

The simple suppression of certain fundamental liberties, or the refusal to apply them, has led to what can be called the refugee phenomenon in Africa. But the agreement signed in 1969 by the OAU does not appear to address this point. The main guarantee given to refugees in Africa is the right of political asylum, that is to say, the right to take refuge in any of the countries which have signed the agreement. But once you have obtained the status of 'refugee', you lose all political rights,[6] and so have no hope of returning to your own country.

A peaceful alternation in power is completely absent from most African constitutions, and the agreement says nothing about this. The OAU appears as 'a league of African leaders determined to stay in power as long as possible, even against the will of the peoples over whose destinies they claim to preside'. It bears a strong resemblance to a trade union. It is indeed regrettable that 'the right of individuals, clear and imprescriptible, be in this way subordinated to the right of the State, which is doubtful and uncertain and generally at the mercy of other interests'.[7]

In the refugee problem, the role of the OAU seems to be completely contradictory. It was created to defend African countries, and supposedly African peoples, but it has practically become an institution to defend the rights of the leaders. The small number of resolutions that it has passed to help the peoples are not even applied. Of course, one of the main preoccupations of every political leader is to preserve law and order, but should they not establish first of all social justice, instead of baptizing as 'order' a state of institutional disorder?

But there's still room for hope. In the family of civilizations governed by laws, Africa is (it seems) the youth of the world, and her law is under the direction of an international law still under formation. So we can hope that the day will come when words and actions go hand in hand for the good of the peoples of the continent.

Notes

1. The Charter of the OAU contains two groups of principles: those which govern the relations of states which are members of the organization, and those which govern the relations between the OAU or one of its members and a third party.

2. This point will be developed below, in the paragraph on the function of the OAU and its contradictions.

3. The presidents respectively of Zaire, Zambia and Angola.

4. This extract is from the second paragraph of the first article of the agreement of the OAU on the specific aspects of the refugee problem in Africa. (Cf. the *Recueil de conventions, accords et arrangements internationaux* about refugees, published by the Delegation of the HCR in Italy, p. 253.)

5. Sam Uba, 'L'exil ou la potence', in *Jeune Afrique*, no. 620.

6. Cf. Article 5 of the agreement of 1969, which formally forbids refugees to 'engage in subversive intrigues', at the risk of losing their status as 'refugees' and being expelled from the country.

7. Claude Julien, in *Le Monde Diplomatique*.

Part 3:
Specific Causes
and Responsibilities

10. War —
In the Horn of Africa

Introduction

The Horn of Africa is the region where the Red Sea, the Indian Ocean and the African continent meet. It is a major cross-roads between the Middle East and Africa, situated close to points which are of vital importance for the world's supply of oil. In this part of the world exist a great number of contradictions or local conflicts: between Ethiopia and Somalia, between Ethiopia and Sudan, between Kenya and Somalia, between the Ethiopian military government and the Eritrean nationalists. Quite apart from the repercussions of neighbouring conflicts or wider issues which make the picture even more complicated: the conflict between Israel and the Arabs, the rivalries between 'progressive' and 'moderate' Arab countries and, on top of it all, the opposition between the superpowers.

The importance of the Horn is so great that in February 1977, some days after the new Ethiopian chief of state took power, Mr Andrew Young, the US representative at the UN, declared: 'What is happening in southern Africa — Angola, Mozambique, Namibia and Zimbabwe — is relatively secondary in relation to what is being prepared in the Horn of Africa' (*L'Unité*, weekly publication of the French Socialist Party, No. 276, December 1977).

Five months later, the biggest conventional war to oppose two African states — Ethiopia and Somalia — was to break out in the desert of Ogaden. The consequences are well known. In support of this confrontation, and at the price of breaking with her most faithful ally in Africa, the Soviet Union settled Ethiopia. The government of Mogadiscio toppled into the western camp and became part of a coalition of the 'moderate' states of the area, sponsored by Saudi Arabia. This was a complete reversal of the situation, which in turn led to a huge 'new deal' in the alliances in the region.

In a context of this kind, where numerous contradictory interests are telescoped, the alliances contracted may easily seem ambiguous and sometimes against nature. Here, more than anywhere else, ideological and religious considerations give way to the nationalist motivations of some of the partners and the necessities of regional geo-politics and world strategy advanced by others. The active support given by Libya and South Yemen (two countries belonging to the 'Front of Resolve') to Ethiopia has never stopped Israel from considering the former Empire of the Negus as the only country in the region which has 'common strategical interests' with the Hebrew state. The arrival of a 'pro-Soviet' government at Addis Ababa has made no changes in the alliance between this country and Kenya, which is a firm ally of the west in this region. They are indeed the only two African states to have concluded a pact of mutual defence . . . aimed at Somalia, which is at the same time an ally of the west and an adept of 'scientific socialism'. Saudi Arabia, which is most certainly an anti-communist country, does not appear unduly embarrassed by the ideology displayed by her Somali ally.

Put off the scent by this imbroglio, and considering the reversal of alliances as the most important fact in the history of the region since 1977, many observers forget the main point: lasting local conflicts and the vicissitudes of the Ethiopian revolution have prepared the region for the action of outside forces. But these are the contradictions, rendered more violent and employed by the superpowers and the powers of the region, which keep the area ablaze, setting loose a crisis without precedent, of which the refugee problem is only a sign.

Why are these Populations in Flight?

The deep causes of this problem are mainly to be sought at the political level. The principal factors which provoke large movements of population throughout the world are well known: the violation of human rights; political and military conflicts within a country; tribal and religious repression; frontier disputes and armed conflicts between neighbouring states; rivalry between the superpowers and regional powers; natural catastrophes; economic crises . . .

All these factors exist in the Horn of Africa and are so interwoven that they result in tragedies of which the drama of the refugees is but a sign. All are clearly not of equal importance. To understand this and to isolate the really determining factors, we shall find it useful to look for the origin of the movement and the way it has developed with the passage of time.

In the Horn the movement of refugees has always been a 'one-way' movement. There are 11,000 Sudanese in Ethiopia, and about 7,000 Zairese, Ugandan and Chadian refugees in Sudan, but with these exceptions, nearly all refugees come from Ethiopia. There are 460,000 of them in Sudan, more than 150,000 in Somalia, 25,000 at Djibouti and nearly 1,600 in Kenya.

As to the evolution of the problem in time, the depopulation began to take on alarming proportions in 1978, when there were 'only' 88,000 refugees in Somalia, 150,000 (most of them Eritreans) in Sudan, hardly more than 1,000 at Djibouti and some hundreds in Kenya. The estimated total was 230,000. Today, the figure of 2,000,000 is certainly an understatement.

This brings up the question of why Ethiopia, or more exactly the military regime in power in Ethiopia, has created more refugees than anywhere else in the world.

At the end of 1977, and in the first few months of 1978, a series of events took place within and without Ethiopia which strengthened the military dictatorship whose politics are at the root of the stream of refugees in the Horn. In March 1978 the Ethiopian army, supported by the Soviets and their allies, succeeded in driving back the Somali invasion. Some months later 'the northern offensive' drove the Eritrean fighters from the large towns they had been occupying for months and obliged them to withdraw to the mountains of the Sahel to the north of Eritrea.

But contrary to popular opinion, it was not the 'conventional' warfare of 1977 and 1978 which set the populations in motion. It was towards the end of these wars, at least in their 'classical' form, that we can note the beginning of what a UN expert has called the 'silent disaster'. The military 'victory' on both fronts is really quite relative, because the guerrilla struggle is still going on. But joined to the defeat suffered by the democratic forces in Ethiopia, it hastened the consolidation of the military bureaucracy in Addis Ababa, which had already begun at the time of the Somali invasion. And the policy adopted by this regime was shortly after to be revealed as the cause of the depopulation not only of the country districts but also of the towns of Ethiopia.

In the country areas, and notably in Eritrea, in Ogaden and in the south of the country, the new government knows that these 'victories' are far from conclusive. That is why it follows them up by a policy of repression, not only to 'punish' civilian populations suspected of sympathy and even of 'collaboration' with enemies of the regime, but also in the hope of preventing any danger of a guerrilla movement supported by these populations. The Dergue undertakes a deliberate policy of 'depopulation' in the disputed regions, and in a lesser degree in Eritrea and in the regions of the south. They bombard the wells, burn the harvests and decimate the cattle. The people are obliged to relocate in what are really 'strategic villages' disguised as 'camps for displaced persons', or to flee the country. A glance at the development of the problem as it has been described by an American doctor shows clearly that this 'scorched earth policy' followed by the Ethiopian military regime is the principal cause of the drama:

> In mid 1978 there were 88,000 refugees in Somali camps, but by mid 1979 the number has risen to 220,000. In the past three months the flight has become a flood tide with over 1,000 new refugees arriving daily. There are now 300,000 refugees in make-shift camps, and American refugee experts in Africa forecast that a million homeless will be in Somali camps within a year.

This same tendency can be observed for the Eritrean refugees.

1978 was the year in which the exodus from country districts began to assume massive proportions, but it was also a turning point for refugees from the towns. The two movements are not unconnected. The nationalist policy of the government is the consequence of the defeats suffered by the Ethiopian democratic forces which controlled the revolutionary movement until the end of 1977.

The first three years of the Ethiopian revolution were not simply marked by the big decrees, the most important of which abolished the centuries-old system of monarchy and feudalism. Supported by a mass movement without precedent in Ethiopian history, millions of peasants, workers and city-dwellers united throughout the country. At the end of 1976 there were 25,000 peasant associations, 1,343 workers' trade unions and more than 2,000 local associations in the towns (kebeles). All these associations, established by democratic elections, were set up as a parallel power facing the former state machinery left by the feudal regime. They provided a democratic alternative to the power of the 'new' civil and military bureaucracy known as the 'Double Power'. This it was which led the anti-democratic forces to install in 1976 the 'white terror', which undertook to do away physically with all the militants behind these organizations.

After having supported the development of these popular forces (more or less wholeheartedly, it is true), the team led by the present head of state, scared by the risks of democratic excesses, toppled as from April 1977 into the camp of 'law and order'. This marks the beginning of 'normalization' in Ethiopia, with the help of the Soviet-Cuban intervention which was rendered possible by the weakening of the patriotic forces. The re-establishment of control led to the dismantling of the organizations of the masses, and was achieved by a massacre which has no precedent in Ethiopian history. The 'scorched earth policy' found its urban equivalent in the 'red terror' which swept down upon all those who resisted in the towns. The repression was massive, severe and indiscriminate against the democratic organizations which had mobilized all those who were favourable to the revolution and national independence. It resulted in 30,000 arrests and thousands of summary executions.

And those who escaped from the terror, students, schoolchildren, intellectuals, civil servants, workers, officers and soldiers, set out in their thousands on the road to exile.

Situation of the Refugees in Host Countries

The refugees in the Horn of Africa are concentrated in very poor countries. The two main host countries, Somalia and Sudan, are among the 31 countries classified as Least Developed Countries (LDC). Djibouti is a tiny country which has no agricultural or industrial resources at all. The socio-economic problems with which these countries are faced are inevitably made worse by the sudden massive influx of refugees. These represent 14% of the population in Djibouti, more than 25% in Somalia and close to 4% in Sudan.

The huge increase of the population would be enough to unsettle the precarious economic and political balance in these countries, but we have also to consider the sociological composition of the groups of refugees. More than 85% of those from rural districts comprise groups of women, children, old people and handicapped persons. As to the men, listen to what an observer of these camps in Somalia has to say:

> The men in these families are gone. Some have been killed in the sputtering Ogaden war, many in bombings and strafing raids that have characterized Cuba's and Russia's contribution to the overt Ethiopian effort at permanently depopulating the contested area. Other men continue to fight in one of the Somali Liberation Front units, while a few remain in the bush with their dying livestock.

A massive arrival of populations, often 'vulnerable', in countries themselves in the grip of economic, political and social difficulties . . . These factors unite to determine the main conditions of existence of refugees in the host countries. There is nevertheless a great diversity in their situations. The needs and the aspirations of young city-dwellers from Addis Ababa or from Asmara are very different from those of nomads from Ogaden or of peasants from the mountains of the north. The problems caused by hosting and installing them are different. For this reason, the case of refugees from the country and those who come from towns must be examined separately.

Refugees from the Country

Nearly 85% of the refugees in the Horn are of rural origin. Their exile is due to the armed conflicts which have destroyed the regions from which they come. The populations cross the frontier and stop in the first place where they feel secure. They tend to settle near the frontier as far as possible, for they hope to go back quickly.

These movements are undertaken hurriedly and in confusion. The refugees settle of their own accord and in disorder, taking no account of the structures established by the governments and the charitable associations to receive them. The regions where they are first received are often remote, and the socio-economic infrastructure is often insufficient. This makes the problem of sending them help more difficult, and the first weeks spent in exile are inevitably the most dramatic. It is made worse by the condition of the refugees who arrive exhausted and so vulnerable to all sorts of sickness. In 1979, after a visit made to a transit camp at the Somali-Ethiopian frontier, an American doctor noted:

> Infectious diseases are rife (malaria, tuberculosis, hepatitis, dysentry and bronchitis), and the potential for a truly decimating epidemic of cholera, for

example, is frighteningly predictable. The death rate is astronomic: in one camp of 41,000 women and children, there had been 2,000 deaths in the last two weeks, and 41 pregnant women died from dysentry during the week I visited the camp.

Once this critical stage has been passed, the authorities and the charitable organizations begin to envisage long-term solutions. Of the three which are theoretically possible, only a resettlement locally seems to be adapted to the uneasy context of the Horn.

Spontaneous repatriation, which would be the ideal solution, remains a remote dream as long as the conflicts continue and the military dictatorship holds sway in Addis Ababa. The self-styled amnesties announced by the Dergue have failed to rouse the enthusiasm of the refugees up to now. The second solution, relocation in the countries of Europe and North America, is difficult to envisage, as these countries prove reluctant to admit even intellectual refugees of urban origin.

The only solution left is to create a local settlement, but this is a difficult and complex undertaking. The aim is to make the refugees self-supporting and allow them to attain a certain standard of living. As most of them come from the country, local resettlement is often conceived as a small unit of agricultural or artisanal projects. Of course, the host countries are unable to finance these projects without risking a delay in their own development. They need international help to succeed. The task is enormous as all the infrastructure (schools, dispensaries and roads) has to be created more or less from nothing. And even when the financing of these autonomous projects is possible, other factors exist which add a new dimension to the problem of helping refugees.

The experience of hosting and installing refugees in Sudan has revealed a certain number of problems which can be considered as characterizing the installation of refugees in all developing countries. They are at the same time economic, political and social problems and have led the Sudanese authorities to define a policy containing the following points:

1) the installation of refugees in any given region must not cause a drop in the living standard of the local population;

2) the assistance received from international sources must not be calculated so as to allow the refugees a higher standard of living than the population of the host country;

3) nor should it prove an incentive to those who have remained in their own country to resort to exile for economic reasons;

4) the infrastructure set up to help the refugees should, as far as possible, also serve the people of the host country;

5) the projects must fit into the regional or national plan of development.

These recommendations were made by the National Committee for

Refugees and accepted by the Sudanese authorities; they are based on political considerations which are easy to understand because they aim at avoiding jealousy between foreigners and nationals. The objective of charitable organizations which help refugees should both be the increase of the assistance given to the people of the host country, and also a better co-ordination between this development effort and that undertaken in favour of refugees.

Refugees from Towns

The urban refugee is above all an individual, and his flight to a neighbouring country is deliberate and organized. He is much more politically aware, more educated and more ambitious than refugees from the country. He is not satisfied to stay in the first place where he feels safe, as they are: he tries to go to a country in Europe or North America or, at least, to reach the capital of the country he has chosen for his exile. This is in order to continue his studies or to find a job corresponding to his training or his social ambitions.

Even if they are fewer in number (15% of the total), urban refugees are a heavy burden for the host countries. In Sudan there are 50,000 living in Khartoum, and out of the 300,000 inhabitants of Port Sudan there are nearly 40,000 refugees. In Djibouti, out of the 42,000 refugees in the country, 24,000 live in the capital. As to Kenya, more than 90% of the 5,000 Ethiopian refugees are to be found at Nairobi. In Somalia, it is known that only a third of the refugee population is living in the camps prepared for them. The others live among the people, in the country, and to a lesser degree in Hargessa and Mogadiscio. Even if it is difficult to give an exact figure, one can say that some tens of thousands of refugees live in urban centres.

This high percentage puts them in competition with the local population. The Sudanese Commissioner for Refugees states: 'Most of these refugees settle of their own accord in the towns, where they have to share medical services, food, water and public transport with the local population. As these services are already insufficient for our own needs, they put a heavy burden on our national economy.'

The sociological composition of urban refugee populations and their legitimate aspiration to social promotion are supplementary factors of competition. Compared with refugees from the country, the proportions of those in the different age groups or those who have an equivalent level of instruction are the reverse. A survey undertaken in Kenya showed that children less than five years of age represent only 13% of the total, while 66% are persons old enough to work (from 18 to 60 years of age). The proportion of the sexes gives two men for one woman. As to their level of instruction, there are only 12% in the group who have had no schooling, whereas 28% have been through primary school, 20% enjoy professional training, 27% come from secondary schools and 13% from higher education.

The typical urban refugee is looking for a job or for training in countries where there is already heavy competition in these fields. How can the host country satisfy refugees' aspirations when its schooling rate is less than 50% and when 40% of its active population is seeking employment, as is the case in Djibouti?

In these conditions it is not surprising that, according to inquiries made at Khartoum, only 5% to 10% of the refugees have got a job. The figure is 14% for Nairobi. As for schooling, the situation is such that the host governments are sometimes obliged to resort to extreme solutions. Thus, in Sudan, the local government of the region of Kassalla, where 11% of the children in primary schools are refugees, has simply forbidden refugee children access to secondary schools. 'The provincial People's Council has adopted a resolution by which refugee children are not allowed to be admitted to intermediate and secondary schools.'

The urban refugee, without work, badly lodged in the poorest quarters of the towns, without regular and sufficient means of subsistence, becomes a prey to serious material and psychological problems. Being uprooted, feeling isolated and uncertain are sentiments experienced by all exiles, but they are even more severely felt by those who come from towns. The host governments can often make them feel more marginal than they already are by accusing them of causing all the shortages, the rise in prices, unemployment and delinquency.

The remedies proposed do not always meet the desires of the people concerned. One of the solutions envisaged consists in transferring them to rural regions where the way of life, farming work, life in a collective and the relations with peasants are new to them. Most of the attempts at imposing this solution have failed, even if the authorities have been led to organize round-ups to relieve the congestion in the towns.

The other solution, which has been tried out in Sudan, is the 'wage-earning settlement', which tries to avoid uprooting the refugees again. They are installed in new quarters established near big towns, where they can work on their own account at the head of a small business, a small industry or an artisanal workshop. This is a reasonable solution, even if the young people and the intellectuals do not consider it as the ideal course. Unable to obtain university training or work corresponding to their professional qualifications, these refugees try to settle in European countries or in North America. But the least that can be said is that these countries are very reluctant to host refugees from Africa. The United States offers them the best chance to make a new start, but in 1981 it accepted less than 3,000 refugees from Africa, although in the same year it received a total of more than 130,000 refugees.

Conclusion

The ideal solution would be voluntary repatriation. But the return home cannot be envisaged until the political causes which were at the origin of the drama have been eliminated. It is evident that, in the complex and troubled context of the Horn of Africa, the struggle for peace and democracy can only advance very slowly. In the interval, all those who feel concerned at the suffering of these populations must continue to increase their help. On this point it is clear that much has yet to be done. Africa, as a 'continent of refugees' has not, until now, received the attention it deserves as a consequence of this unhappy privilege. As an executive of the UN HCR stated: 'The average share of international assistance which goes to an African refugee is US$22, whereas refugees from elsewhere receive on the average US$56.'

It becomes less and less easy to justify this situation since the human-itarian organizations working in the field become more and more conscious of the new dimensions of the refugee problem in African countries.

As we have seen above, helping refugees implies a larger notion of sharing with the nationals of the host countries. Let us see what a representative of the non-governmental organizations in Sudan declared at a Conference on Refugees, held at Khartoum in September 1982:

> We believe that there is little or no distinction between the refugees and a large segment of the Sudanese people in regard to sharing pain, suffering, depriva-tion and the 'urge to live'. We cannot compartmentalize our genuine and abiding concern for the Sudanese people and for the plight of the refugees. Our concern is indivisible. We attempt to extend assistance in equal measure for we believe in a Sudanese community that is based on mutual respect and mutual recognition of the particular needs of the different groups living in the Sudan.

From this it becomes clear that beyond the humanitarian aspect, assistance to refugees in developing countries must be integrated into the wider view of the development of these countries.

'There is now an increasing awareness within the international com-munity that the traditional distinction between humanitarian relief and development assistance needs to be reviewed.' The Pan-African Confer-ence on the Situation of Refugees in Africa which was held at Arusha (Tanzania) in 1979 is more explicit. Point 10 of the final declaration underlined that idea by affirming: 'The Conference stresses that the programme covering rural refugees should be planned and implemented within the context of national, sub-regional and regional endeavours.'

It is only by giving a positive response to these different problems that the international community can accept the challenge launched by the 'silent disaster' which more than two million refugees are now enduring in the Horn of Africa.

11. Apartheid — Southern Africa

The task force started by listening to evidence on the situation of refugees in southern Africa. Our witness, a citizen of Swaziland, began by insisting on the fact that all the problems in the region were more or less consequences of the regime of South Africa and the institutionalized policy of apartheid. The discussion group put a strong accent on the importance of recognizing this fact as the principal cause of trouble in this part of Africa.

The policy of South Africa leads to consequences of two kinds: a massive production of refugees, both inside South Africa and outside the country; the precarious situation of these refugees when they are living in neighbouring countries.

80% of the refugees come from the towns; the reasons for their exile are political and not economic. The term 'refugee' is strictly applied to these political exiles who have left their country because the South African laws on security make their living conditions impossible. They are hunted by the police and if they wanted to return home they would be arrested immediately and imprisoned for life or accused under the anti-terrorist security laws. For the moment, the term is not applicable to the millions of Africans who have been chased from their homes and lodged in the Bantustans. Of these we shall speak later. It would indeed be damaging to those who engaged in the struggle to confound in the same group those who are political refugees in the strict sense of the term and the people parked in the Bantustans.

Those who leave the country for political motives explain their decision in this way: South Africa, a country engaged in civil war, uses her defence force, a very strong military corps, against the freedom movements and more especially against the African National Congress (ANC) and its armed branch, Umkonto we Sizwe. With the moral and technological support of the western countries, especially the US under the Reagan administration and thanks to his policy of offensive alliances, South Africa is heavily armed. It is also a state which applies the ideology of national security, preaching a total strategy to thwart 'the world uprising of communism'. Politically, South Africa is thus in an explosive situation.

The tides of refugees from South Africa and Namibia, which is still illegally controlled by South Africa, move towards Botswana, Lesotho, Swaziland, Mozambique and Angola. But these states cannot practise a real policy of reception because of the lack of infrastructure (sanitary, educational, etc.) or of economic means but also because they fear the military reprisals of South Africa,[1] and because they depend upon that country.

In the last ten years the situation of refugees has become worse and worse. Before this, the host countries used to allow refugees to stay on their territory for several years, but now they are replacing this system by a more precarious form of transit. And the personal security of the refugees is less and less assured: witnesses report numerous cases of kidnapping, bombing and imprisonment, not to mention the refusal to receive refugees.

The direct attacks made by South Africa on neighbouring states who receive political refugees make it more and more difficult for these refugees to survive, even outside South Africa. Examples could be given of what happens in Lesotho, Mozambique, Zimbabwe, Botswana or Swaziland, where South Africa uses every kind of tactic to terrorize these countries and prevent them from receiving those who are in flight for political reasons.

Leaving aside these refugees to whom the official definition applies,[2] we must examine the case of those Black South Africans who have been refugees in their own country since the creation of the Bantustans.

This policy, organized by Vorster, represents one of the most diabolical systems of exploitation. Officially, apartheid is presented in the following way: 'South Africa is made up of several races. It is difficult for different peoples to live together, so we will give them the opportunity to live separately: each race will pursue its development without impeding the others, and everybody will be happier.'

The literal translation of the word 'apartheid' is 'separate development'. So the Black South Africans live cut off from the rest of the population, and only have the right to vote in the Bantustans. The Indians and the Coloureds have been reincorporated by the White man's parliamentary system under the recent new constitutional proposals.

The government claims that the complex situation in South Africa is due to British colonial policy in the 19th Century. In answer to questions asked by a Third World group in August 1977, the South African ambassador in Paris wrote: 'It has now become necessary to destroy what the British have done and to decolonize South Africa completely. That means drawing frontiers between the different nations and the establishment of independent national states.'

This propaganda is not supported by facts: the Africans are divided into ten linguistic groups, counting the Xhosa people, which is itself divided into two groups, the Ciskei Xhosa and the Transkei Xhosa. But against this Black population, the Whites are mobilized as a single unit, despite similar differences of language.

This population is submitted to unreasonable and exasperating laws which control their movements. It is obligatory to carry a 'permission to circulate', like dogs carrying a plate with their owner's name. If they haven't got their plate, they are arrested. On the economic level, the Blacks account for 70% of the total population, but only 13% or 14% of the land surface is allocated to them. This land is divided among the Bantustans, which are separated into 270 zones scattered throughout the country. Only the Transkei, the first Bantustan to be established, forms a more or less homogeneous territory. Development is so slow in these areas that the so-called independence seems more like a sinister farce. The Bantustans are extremely poor and unproductive, deprived of all mineral or industrial resources.

This shows clearly the aim pursued by the policy. Obliged to reside in the Bantustans, the Blacks cannot find work on the spot and are forced to take jobs in the 'White' zones where they are exiles and have no rights. The firms have not built their installations inside the Bantustans, but just outside them. They made no mistake!

From the social point of view, the Africans are subject to the law on Bantu education. Since it was passed in the 1950s, the Blacks have received an education which keeps them in their place as a source of servile manpower for the Whites. The system of separate public and private services for education is felt to be particularly degrading.

These injustices have led to armed struggle and increased the mobilization of the Blacks and their opposition to the regime and the system of production. The struggle for alternative economic structures and for political power is getting fiercer, and many young people leave the country to join the armed branch of the ANC and receive political instruction.

The responsibility of South Africa and the western countries which support her is considerable, but we should not ignore the role played by China in this part of Africa.

China has never recognized SWAPO and the ANC, which muster the freedom fighters, even if recently there has been the beginning of a dialogue. In Angola, from 1963 to 1973, when the country became independent, China supported UNITA and the FNLA of Roberto Holden, giving these movements financial assistance against the troops of the MPLA. Even now, and despite the help which these movements receive from America, China continues to back this side.

We now know the price which the nationalist movements and Angola have paid in the struggle against apartheid. There are 70,000 Namibians living in exile in neighbouring countries, without mentioning the thousands who are nomads in the region, and we can affirm that from 1963 until today China has indirectly contributed, in southern Africa, to help support the apartheid system.

The help China has accorded to the ZANU liberation movement in Zimbabwe has always been conditioned by a fierce ideological struggle against the forces of ZAPU, despite the fact that they are allies in the national front, because the latter are supported by the socialist countries. The result is that ZAPU has been bled to death, and that the Matabeles who formed the majority of their supporters have been obliged to take refuge in Zambia and the neighbouring countries.

The attitude taken by China towards the South African invasion of Angola was so impudent that Tanzania felt obliged to make things clear by closing the entrance to the port of Dar-es-Salaam where the Chinese were wanting to unload supplies for UNITA.

China claims to be anti-imperialist. In fact, for reasons based on her internal strategy and on her 'anti-imperialist' tactics (which need a deeper analysis), she is always on the side of the anti-nationalist forces. And this is the reason why internal quarrels between opposing factions of the liberation movements have provoked vast movements of the population from Zaire towards Zimbabwe via Angola.

And the latest confrontations in Zimbabwe between the Zimbabwean army and what is left of the armed forces of ZAPU, which took place at the beginning of 1983, provoked yet another exodus of the population.

Some Recommendations

Faced with this discouraging picture of the situation of refugees in Southern Africa, the study group felt compelled to formulate the following recommendations:

1) The western countries are largely responsible for the situation, by their well-nigh unconditional support of the South African regime. This support seems even to be on the increase. Our first recommendation is then: That actions be developed to bring to a halt the support given by western governments to South Africa. We realize that a rupture of western economic relations with this country, because of what it would cost, makes it necessary to make a huge effort to mobilize western public opinion. This means that we need a massive campaign of information and sensitization directed to the wider public through the media, organizations and agencies specialized in these questions. This book would like to contribute to this.

2) During our investigation, education has little by little emerged as a main priority. That means:
● welcoming African students in western universities. Stress was put on the danger which underlies the proclamation: 'Africans will have to live in Africa.' We do not deny that this should be the principal long-term objective, but we believe it can only be achieved and justified when they have obtained the necessary competence;
● developing African universities;
● strengthening research units on African soil;
● and developing programmes of education with a special regard for refugees.

This would serve as a preventive measure, giving these populations a better opportunity to become aware of the facts and to decide for themselves the course of action to follow. This point is in parallel with the following recommendation.

3) We should support organizations working in Africa for refugees, be they humanitarian, ecumenical or groups fighting for liberation. Support should especially be given to the formation of those who are fighting for freedom within South Africa.

4) We should stress the need to develop African non-governmental organizations which can work in the field together with the international organizations of the same type. This seems the only way to assure that knowledge of field conditions and of the populations concerned be linked with well-established and recognized financial and technical bases, and that the necessary changes be made on the spot in the structures and the mentalities.

The global orientation of these first four points then led us to formulate the last two recommendations:

5) The French and other western governments should be encouraged:
- to increase their support for African refugees and the help they give them, both by receiving them at home and helping them where they are now living.
- to give stronger support to freedom movements which try to help refugees.

6) This seminar should be brought to its logical conclusion: the definition of a project and the creation of a committee with practical responsibility:
- for acquiring accurate information on the problems of the region, but information which is also independent and which can be made known in Africa and in the western world;
- for creating or supporting the infrastructure necessary for education in the field. This will appear as a final project at the end of the book.[3]

Notes

1. See Appendix 1, p. 137ff.
2. We think this definition can be criticized; see Chapter 13.
3. Cf. pp. 122–3.

12. Class Oppression Replacing Imperial Domination — in East and Central Africa

If we wish to understand all the implications of the refugee phenomenon in Africa, especially in the eastern part of Central Africa, we must go beyond the general causes and responsibilities and discuss those which are peculiar to this region, sometimes even to each one of the countries concerned.

One of these causes is the use made of local bourgeoisies as relays for imperialism. While according these states a fictional independence and eliminating the nationalists which caused trouble, the colonial powers 'created from nothing' local bourgeoisies, on which they could count to allow them to continue the complete exploitation of the natural riches of their countries.

Once in power, these bourgeoisies got down to tracking wherever they could those of their nationals who had taken refuge in neighbouring countries. Zaire and Burundi are good examples of this kind of situation.

International imperialism has never accepted that Zaire (ex-Belgian Congo), whose natural resources have been called 'a geological scandal', should become truly independent, as that would mean losing the uranium and other strategic raw materials which can be mined in this country. That is why a national bourgeoisie was methodically put into power.

The Establishment of a National Bourgeoisie in Zaire

Faced with the bitter failure of the 'moderate' party in the national elections, colonization retreated to Katanga (now Shaba), one of the richest regions in Africa. At the time of the secession of Katanga, colonization (or to put it more clearly: international imperialism) succeeded in expelling from power and finally eliminating the nationalist leader Lumumba with some of the members of his party. All Lumumba's friends were to be pursued in the town of Léopoldville (now Kinshasa) so as to establish a phantom government. This is an exact description of the Iléo government and of the College of General Commissioners who were to govern in the midst of chaos which rendered possible all kinds of dirty tricks.

A group of conspirators was created to fight against the nationalism advocated by the former prime minister, Patrice Lumumba, to reconcile the public opinion of the country with foreign interests, and to gain the control of all the key positions in the country with the help of the national army, which had remained faithful to the commander-in-chief, Mobutu. All means were acceptable for the Group of Binza to discourage nationalism: assassination, torture, arbitrary witnesses. National reconciliation was brought about in the most favourable conditions for the 'moderate' party, supported in the wings by the Group of Binza.

This group became more important than the government of the republic and even outstripped the chief of state. Under the presidency of General Mobutu, it counted among its principal members Nemdaka, administrator of the National Police Force and supposedly a member of the CIA, Bomboko, Minister of Foreign Affairs, and Ndele, governor of the National Bank . . . When the government of Tshombé took power, neo-colonialism officially took its place in the country with its mercenary troops, who were to massacre the revolutionaries in the east of the country and in the Kwilu. And that was the moment chosen by Mobutu to seize power.

The Organized Hunt for Revolutionary Elements

Once in power Mobutu defined his priorities: first, to follow up the work undertaken by Tshombé within the country; secondly, to track down the members of the opposition who had taken refuge in neighbouring countries.

As to the first objective, Mobutu preached his famous policy of pacification, but continued to massacre the revolutionaries who had refused to leave for the surrounding countries. He soon achieved this objective with the help of the mercenaries of Tshombé and of the CIA. As to the second objective, Mobutu undertook a so-called policy of good neighbour relations, the aim of which was really to facilitate the destruction of the small groups of resisters who had taken refuge in the surrounding countries. With a few exceptions, among which are Tanzania and Angola, these Zairese citizens living abroad will be obliged to return to Zaire.

Once it has the situation in hand, both outside and inside Zaire, imperialism will make extraordinary profits. It has even gone so far as to designate a zone in the centre of the country to be given over to nuclear experiments (the Otrag concern). The economy is entirely in the hands of the national bourgeoisie, which is at the service of imperialism. The Zairese economy is the most open of African economies: everything produced in the country is exported, while essential objects are all imported.

What Does 'Sanctuary' Mean in Africa?
(Analysis by a Rwandese refugee of the case of his compatriots living in Kenya, Tanzania, Uganda, Zaire and Burundi)

The Reasons Behind the Exile

The refugees from Rwanda were among the first refugees in Africa — in the wave of refugees which we are considering. The first stream of them left the country at the end of November 1959. The genocide went on until 1962, and many tens of thousands were obliged to seek sanctuary in the neighbouring states: Burundi, Uganda, Tanzania, Zaire and, later, Kenya.

The first tribal massacres took place before the declaration of national independence on 1 July 1962. Rwanda was still under the Belgian mandate together with her southern neighbour, and still formed part of the territory of Rwanda-Urundi. From a legal point of view it is justified to ask what was the responsibility of Belgium, as it was under the colonial administration that the violence first broke out and that the first refugees fled. And indeed, many documents show that the Belgian authorities, instead of stopping the massacre, failed to honour their undertakings towards the UN which could have lessened the tension, even if it could not have avoided the rise of violence. A UN mission asked in vain that the authorities bring back the refugees to their country before organizing the first elections and according independence to Rwanda. We should keep in mind the repressive measures taken from 1959 to 1962 against the Tutsi alone: the campaign of intimidation against the victims of the burning of the refugee camps of Myamata, in the south-east of Rwanda (the refugees were in their own country!); the massive arrests; the intervention of air-borne Belgian parachutists from the military bases in Congo . . . The 'Paracommandos and the head-cutter (helicopter)' have left traumatic legends on the hills of Rwanda.

Rwanda is a state formed by the progressive union of formerly independent tribal units. The process of unification accelerated from the end of the 15th Century, when wars of conquest sometimes brought in territories outside the present boundaries of Rwanda. The present frontiers were traced by agreement between the colonial powers, and the state of Rwanda reduced to an area of 26,338 sq. km (approximately 10,170 sq. miles). Before the 'tribal' conflict broke out, three social groups, the Batutsi, the Bahutu and the Batwa, lived together in cultural harmony using the same language, the same social institutions and the same customs. As is often the case in Black Africa, the three groups had economic roles which were relatively specialized.

For several centuries the Batwa were hunters and potters, but by the colonial epoch they were only potters, as the forest had been cut down long before. They now constitute a marginal group in the country, separated from the rest of the population and living outside their villages. The Bahutu and the Batutsi were generally farmers and herdsmen, but the Tutsi exercised a preponderant role in politics. We should not however assimilate the mass of the Batutsi to this political aristocracy (as the propaganda of the 1960s had an abusive tendency to do), as they were completely immersed in a mass which also contained the Batwa and the Bahutu, who had no political responsibility.

The unity of the nation was based on a cultural and linguistic similarity which deserves note as, if we put aside the Burundi, this is very rare in Africa. This unity was also strengthened by a monarchical ideology which is deeply rooted in the minds of the Rwandese people. All the institutions which governed the Rwanda, up to the two republics which have held power successively, are the fruit of the idea the people had of their country, which was closely associated with their king.

Of course this ancient form of socio-political organization was the source of inequalities, some of which are at the root of the conflict between the Tutsi and the Hutu peoples. But it would be wrong to neglect the ideological foundations of this quarrel, which was propagated in the school manuals and by former ethnographical studies. The Batwa are presented as pygmies who spend their time looking for fruits and chasing animals: they are a sorry race, described in terms we should today call 'racist'. The Bahutu appear as pioneer farmers, forming a group of drudges (this theme was specially developed after independence), while the Batutsi were shown as the 'noble conquerors from the Nile Valley', whose cultural superiority came from the very depths of civilization itself.

There exists a stereotyped literature about the Tutsi, which constitutes an excellent example of the falsification of African history and its consequences. This carries an ideology which can be read several ways: one interpretation, where the Tutsi are represented as a people from outside Africa, has been considerably developed in the work of contemporary historians. An article worth consulting on this subject was published by one of the specialists of the region in which Rwanda is situated, under the title 'False Blacks', in *Le Monde* of 28 June 1981.

From the point of view of the first Belgian ethnologists and administrators, the Tutsi must have been a 'superior race' to impose (*sic*!) 'the monarchy peacefully on the other two races'! From this were drawn an abundance of racist theories of this type: 'the Bantu peoples (of which the Hutu in Rwanda are a branch) are distinguished by the drowsiness in which their intelligence has remained . . . whereas the Batutsi, a ruling race of giants, are far more apt to command and much more organized than the Bantu . . .'

This natural disposition was claimed for them on the basis of their supposed 'descent from the Semites'. 'Distant descendants of Noah by the accursed branch of Ham, they were supposed to have arrived in Rwanda later than the others.' In this way is insinuated another reading of Rwandese history, in which they are foreigners. The Hutu leaders made good use of this theme during the campaign against the Tutsi, first of all during the political crisis of 1959 which provoked the first wave of refugees, and later at different stages of the tribal conflict. In the years before independence those who had earlier proclaimed the 'racial' (*sic*) superiority of the Tutsi began with as much conviction to denounce them as the greatest danger Rwanda had ever known: they were 'traitors' (to what cause?), 'agents working under the orders of Moscow, foreigners who should be sent back to their home in Abyssinia . . .' So did the administrators and the parish priests become, in large numbers, apostles of violence.

The analysis of this ideology of the 'Tutsi, conquering unbelievers' only completes that which is founded on purely politico-economic facts. It highlights the ideas which guided the men who were set against the Tutsi at the time all this happened, as well as the idea of them held by countries which have given them asylum, and which count in their population tribes which are culturally close to those in Rwanda. This analysis explains the rapidity with which the homes of the Tutsi were set ablaze, while it also allows us to understand the clear conscience of the authorities of Rwanda faced with the drama of their compatriots turned refugees. They are 'foreigners, in any case . . .', according to certain political leaders in Rwanda.

That is how the first national leaders publicly justified their seizure of power, while the Belgians were setting up the first vindictive government of the Parmehutu (the sole party, overthrown by the military coup d'état in 1973, together with the regime which it had set in power). The violent slogans that were to be heard in the songs broadcast by the radio all day long testify to the hatred of foreigners which was a characteristic of the conflict: 'Strike the serpents [the Tutsi]. Break their heads. Send them back home, to Abyssinia . . .'

This campaign against the Tutsi was in full sway when in 1963 some armed refugees tried to re-enter their country by force. The attack was limited to a small sector of the frontier between Rwanda and Burundi, but it was enough to justify another wave of physical violence. Several thousand Tutsis perished at Nyamata. The police made new arrests in the urban centres, and there has up to now been no news of many people imprisoned since 1963. It is known that some have died in prison, but the fate of the vast majority of the captives is still a mystery, especially of those who underwent treatment in the special prison of Ruhengeri, on which no serious information has ever been available.

It seems that the regime of President Kayibanda has always justified the repression and the massacres on the grounds that they were reprisals designed to make the Tutsi in exile think twice before engaging in guerrilla warfare. The Tutsi still living in the country were made virtual hostages, as their security depended on a complete rupture of their relations with those of their fellow-tribesmen who were refugees outside the country. But in 1973 it became clear that this relative security could be jeopardized at any moment, even when the Hutu leaders were fighting among themselves for power.

Wanting to get rid of troublesome rivals, especially since they had got into positions in the army, President Kayibanda and his political friends built up a scenario of troubles in the schools and managed to create a new climate of hatred against the Tutsi. The young Hutu attacked the Tutsi in the towns, before spreading the violence over the hills, as the police and the army did not react, and their leaders, hoping that the government would be overthrown, looked favourably on their inactivity.

These are the circumstances in which the last wave of Rwandese refugees left the country, known to the former exiles as the 'men of 73'.

Problems Faced by the Refugees Today

Refugees from Rwanda are unequally spread out in the neighbouring countries. The estimates which are generally published by the humanitarian organizations give from 200,000 to 250,000 in Burundi, from 78,000 to 80,000 in Uganda, from 36,000 to 40,000 in Tanzania, about 22,000 in Zaire and more than 2,000 in Kenya. But we should bear in mind that these are the figures given for those who receive help from the HCR of the UN, and they say nothing of those who have managed to obliterate (for reasons it is easy to understand) all mention of their status as foreigners. Some refugees from Rwanda have relatives who have already emigrated, generally for economic reasons, and have made a home in the neighbouring state. These have often been able to join their family and disappear among the local population. But that has not been achieved without raising serious problems of a socio-economic or a political nature, or without modifying the relations between these Rwandese and the peoples of the host country. The situation of the refugees from Rwanda varies from country to country.

A Small Minority Screened from the Tensions

The 4,000 or so refugees to be found in Europe or in Kenya are doubtless the only ones who are really sheltered from ill will and social tensions. In Europe they are for the most part students who, at the end of their studies, are going to go back and settle down in Africa.

The fraction settled in Kenya is mainly composed of people living as artisans or tradesmen. They earn barely enough to keep their families alive. It doesn't seem that these refugees living in Kenya have any reason to fear threats to their security at the present time. Doubtless they do not form a group large enough to become noticeable in society, and also it is easier to live unnoticed in the large urban agglomeration of Nairobi than in a small city centre in Burundi or Zaire.

The Refugees in Tanzania

At the present time, the question of Rwandese refugees seems to have found a solution. An administrative measure has been taken in favour of them and has allowed for the naturaliztion of 36,000 Rwandese refugees. This answers the wishes of those who find an official integration is a solution to their problem, and their point of view is reasonable, as it takes into account the demographic and economic factors (over-population and poverty) which are invoked by the Rwandese authorities to oppose demands for repatriation. But the greater portion of the refugees wish to return to their country and plead their cause with the following arguments:

They declare first of all their opposition to any measure of naturalization which is obligatory, or negotiated by the Rwandese government without asking their advice, as had been the case. The naturalization of the 36,000 Rwandese by the Tanzanian government was decided in exchange for a large financial participation on the part of Rwanda in the construction of a hydroelectrical plant in the valley of the Kagera, a project which will benefit the western districts of Tanzania first of all. Some of the refugees go as far as saying that they have been 'sold'. A second set of arguments draws on the fact that in Africa the law is fragile: 'We have already been naturalized in Uganda', we hear some say, 'are we not pushed out today and driven to despair?' And that leads us to the last of the disillusions of the Rwandese refugees.

Those who are Thrown Out of Uganda

A little history is necessary if we are to understand the Rwandese problem in Uganda. And we shall have to remember certain historical facts to understand the situation of the refugees in Zaire, as in each case some members of the Rwandese community are not refugees and there is a further problem of political frontiers which do not correspond to cultural frontiers.

In the south of Uganda, notably in the region of Kigezi which is crossed by a range of volcanoes (the 'Virunga'), a population of Rwandese culture, language and tradition has been living under Ugandan sovereignty since the beginning of the century. The Ugandan Bakiga were separated by the colonial frontiers set up between 1885 and 1910 from the Bakiga who live in Rwanda. This geo-political separation has never stopped regular communications between the two peoples, and the Bakiga have friends and relatives on both sides of the frontier.

This situation is a possible cause of conflicts, of the kind that can break out on many other African borders. But there is also a situation where immigrants resident in Uganda for one or two generations have acquired rights which are now recognized. When Uganda was under British administration, her agricultural economy was prosperous, and tens of thousands of Rwandese citizens, threatened by the famines which regularly struck their country, or fleeing from the forced labour to which their colonial administration subjected them in order to build roads, crossed the border seeking work in the plantations. After 1920, to go to Uganda represented the only hope for many Rwandese peasants of finding the money they needed to get married or simply to pay the head-tax. Thousands of families renounced any intention of returning to their native country. These immigrants then joined those who had become Ugandan by the fact of the colonial frontier and formed the tribe called Banyarwanda, or literally, the people of Rwanda.

According to an article published in the daily paper *Le Monde* on 1 December 1982, under the title: 'The drama of an expelled minority' (the

Rwandese), the constitution of Uganda guarantees Ugandan nationality to all the Banyarwanda born before independence. But we have to realize that texts of law have no greater value than the paper on which they are written. We shall come back to this problem when talking about the problem of Rwandese refugees in Zaire. Right now, it is more important to examine the political aspect of the question.

The international press and some local organs (especially in Rwanda) have explained the conflicting points of view. The Ugandan government claims that it is simply a spontaneous repatriation of the Banyarwanda, who had refused to leave their homes to move to another region. The Rwandese authorities say the people thrown out in October 1982 were all Ugandan refugees, and it is on this basis that Rwanda has appealed to the international organizations and to the United States for help. Later, probably because a highly critical journal (called the *Kinyamateka*, a church monthly which enjoys considerable moral prestige) had drawn attention to a high percentage of Rwandese among the refugees, the Rwandese government was obliged to recognize that 6,000 of them were indeed citizens of Rwanda.

It seems that those who are counted in this figure are almost exclusively Hutu. But how could one distinguish between true and false Rwandese in a population speaking the national language, the Kinyarwanda? On the basis of identity cards, it is claimed, because they carry the mention of the tribe of origin (Hutu, Tutsi or Twa) since colonial times!

This is the official explanation, but it doesn't stand close examination. First of all, the return was not spontaneous, as the government of Kampala has affirmed. This is simply a fiction, invented afterwards and in flagrant contradiction with the observations of the international press. There is no doubt that these Rwandese had been brutalized and even, in a lesser degree, submitted to physical violence. They fled at the behest of the highest functionaries of the state and the party, after soldiers had sacked the dwellings of some of them and plundered all on their passage (cf. the article quoted from *Le Monde*, 1 December 1982).

In the statement of considerations preceding these different articles the legislator has taken care to say clearly that the naturalization only

In the middle of September, three militant members of the Party in power were killed during a confused skirmish with soldiers of the national army and some Rwandese. This was called 'a plot against the Party' and set the country on fire. The expulsion of the Rwandese began on 30 September, under the control of the local Party chiefs and the local authorities. The victims were all the Rwandese established in the district of East Ankole (Mbarara). Families which had been living in the region since 1927 were expelled and deprived of their goods. Here and there the houses were burnt or pillaged, and herds of cattle, sheep or goats were stolen. In a few days thousands of refugees were on the roads with nowhere to go. In the 1960s the refugees were able to go to the camps, but these are now overpopulated and the people who are in charge of them are overwhelmed. The High Commission for Refugees at the United Nations has promised to intervene next week.

Even more trustworthy is the evidence given by the French doctors who were a part of the team of Doctors Without Frontiers which was sent to the improvised refugee camps in Rwanda or to the Belgian section of Assistance to Displaced Persons (ADP). In a letter to its supporters, the Management Council of the ADP related in these terms the impression of a member of the section who was sent to bring these refugees help from the HCR:

> It is a huge additional task, but a very important one, to help these poor refugees who sleep in the open air, under the trees, in the rain, and live in pitiful conditions. It is the first time in my life that I have seen so much misery, and all that is the result of human stupidity, racial hatred and injustice.

The injustice is that peasants who understand nothing of the political rivalries of the principal Ugandan leaders have to foot the bill for the chaos prevalent in the former republic of Amin Dada. Milton Obote was put in power by elections which were gerrymandered during the occupation of the country by the Tanzanian army. That is why he is opposed, especially by the Baganda and the Banyankole. He has tried to intimidate the rebel populations by repression against the Banyarwanda. He reproaches them for their sympathy (real or presumed) for Yoweri Museveni, a candidate who opposed him in the elections of 1980, and who is now the leader of guerrilla forces fighting against the government. The Rwandese refugees are constantly exposed to this kind of political manoeuvre. If some of them have become members of the local bourgeoisie, the whole community will pay heavily for it. The danger is also to be feared in countries where as yet the authorities have not threatened the Rwandese with expulsion.

The Uncertainty of the Banyarwanda in Zaire
The Rwandese who are living in Zaire are confronted with a problem in many respects comparable with that facing the Banyarwanda of Uganda. In the eastern region of the state (notably Rutshuru and Goma) populations speaking Kinyarwanda have been living since the 18th or the beginning of the 19th Centuries. These Banyarwanda, peripheral with respect to the territory of Rwanda, were left outside the national frontiers established between 1885 and 1910. As well as the waves of spontaneous emigration caused by natural calamities, Rwanda furnished a large number of workers to the mining camps of the Belgian Congo. When both the Congo and the territory of Rwanda-Urundi were part of the same economic unit, the settling of people from Burundi or Rwanda in Congo went unquestioned. And as there was no close definition of nationality, the Congolese and the populations of Rwanda-Urundi were alike called 'natives'. Indeed many administrative reports from this period mention the fact that 'the term "native" has no exact juridical definition.'

These Banyarwanda, introduced into the country long ago, to whom we can add the refugees who arrived in 1959 and 1960, ought to be considered as fully-fledged Zairese citizens. But as we have already seen, laws in Africa can be understood in many ways. Two texts have been published which defined the conditions in which the Rwandese acquired Zairese citizenship:

sole article of the law of 26 March 1971:

> The persons native of Rwanda-Urundi established in Congo on 30 June, 1960 are considered as having acquired Congolese nationality on the above-mentioned date.
> (signed) J. D. Mobutu

article 15 of a law published in the Gazette of the Republic of Zaire, 13th year, no. 1 of 2 January 1972:

> The persons native of Rwanda-Urundi who were established in the province of Kivu on 1 January 1950, and who have continued since then to reside in the Republic of Zaire until the promulgation of the present law, have acquired the Zairese nationality on 30 June 1960.

In the statement of considerations preceding these different articles the legislator has taken care to say clearly that the naturalization only affects 'the natives of Rwanda-Urundi established in the province of Kivu by decision of the colonial authority . . .' How is this attention to detail to be explained? Whatever the true reasons may be, it is clear that it excludes the refugees.

Nobody could have anticipated that this measure, in favour of a category of Rwandese, was to be put back into the melting-pot less than ten years later. The text of the project of 1981 for the Constitution annuls the two preceding laws in the first paragraph of its article 9 of section III. Paragraph 1 of section II specifies in its article 4, after carefully distinguishing the populations who speak the language of Rwanda but became Congolese by annexation in colonial times and ordinary immigrants from Rwanda: 'In the terms of article 11 of the Constitution every person is Zairese who has in his ancestry a member of one of the tribes established on the territory of the Republic of Zaire in its limits of 1 August, 1885, as they have been modified by subsequent conventions.'

The effects of this law, added to the animosity which is now felt towards the Rwandese, can only give rise to a keen anxiety. It seems that we should ask clearly if there is not behind this hostility a much broader political design. Several indications should be taken seriously, but we will mention only two attendant circumstances which threaten grave consequences.

The first is a famous letter attributed to the Rwandese which was sent to the Secretary General of the United Nations as well as to the Secretary of the OAU. This letter calls for the autonomy, and later the independence, of a state embodying the zones of Goma, Rutchuru, Walikalé, Masisi, Kalehé and the island of Ijwi. A zone is the equivalent of a rural district, but on the scale of the country it often occupies a very large sector. It is in these regions that the Banyarwanda live. The document is clearly a forgery. A long enquiry allows us to affirm that it is of Zairese fabrication, in the purest style of the famous 'Protocols of the Sages of Zion'.

After this letter had been widely circulated in Zaire, the students of the university campus of Bukavu produced another note, claiming it had been extracted from a vast 'Plan for a Tutsi colonization in the Kivu', elaborated in the 1960s. This text was attached to a long tract which starts with the words: 'Long live the Zairese nation! Death to those who usurp our nationality!'

We extract from this document a few passages of terrifying violence:

> It is now twenty-two years [1962 is the year in which the 'Plan' was supposed to have started going round in Tutsi emigration circles] since a group of refugees undertook shameful and deceptive manoeuvres in order to obtain, by force or by ruse, Zairese nationality and to enjoy all the advantages which belong to a real Zairese citizen . . . And now these impostors, having usurped our nationality, are seeking the autonomy on our soil of certain parts of Zairese territory.
>
> The students had organized official demonstrations to express their dissent . . . Blood was shed and the local authorities had to refer the matter to the higher levels of government.
>
> We send out an alarm call to all authentic Zairese citizens, worthy of our nationality, calling them to join us to fight against these Nyenzi, these poisonous serpents, the Tutsi of the Rwanda who have emigrated to Zaire.
>
> These people are thrown out everywhere, but they occupy our public places, they have acquired high responsibilities in our government so as to dig their heels in more firmly. These hated people even want to cut into the geography of our country . . .

There is no need to go on quoting from this literature. We can only hope that the tension calms down, and that hatred will not get the better of reason.

The Frustration of the Refugees in Burundi

It is in Burundi that the Rwandese refugees seem to have found the warmest welcome. At least if we can believe a petition signed by some of them and sent to the 'International Colloquium on the Protection of African Refugees' organized at Dakar from 12 to 15 December 1982. The signatories of this document state: 'Up to now, Burundi has reserved a kind welcome to Rwandese refugees. No violent events have taken place to disturb their settling in.'

Indeed the government of Burundi helped the refugees for a long time, especially in the fields of education and work. The primary and secondary schools were open to young Rwandese on the same conditions as to the people of the country. A certain number of refugees were able to pursue and finish their studies in the University of Burundi, and have subsequently taken up positions both in the public and the private sector.

That happened, say certain inhabitants of Burundi, during the presidency of Micombero, who was accused of being too lax and removed from office by a military coup d'état in 1976. The new regime has put a stop to the flow of naturalizations on which the preceding government had engaged. There are several reasons for this, some of which are simply subjective: a number of citizens are jealous of the success of the Rwandese. But some are objective and seem justified.

If we examine the situation seriously, there is no doubt that Burundi is as poor and as highly populated as Rwanda, who objects to the repatriation of her refugees on grounds of poverty and over-population. Faced with serious economic difficulties, the Burundese government found it necessary to put limits to her policy of helping refugees: in the schools, a quota has been fixed for the Rwandese, restricting the number of children who receive schooling; to be admitted they have to get a mark 20% above that needed for the children who are citizens. On the job market, the Rwandese are of course up against the general crisis, but the government has taken some very restrictive measures towards them. The result is that when the refugees compare their present situation to that they were in before, they feel a certain frustration and say: 'Nobody cares for us.' In Bujumbura, the capital, where the pick of the Rwandese refugees live, a certain restlessness is to be observed. Even simple tradesmen feel they are touched by a restriction which was thought at first to hit only civil servants and representatives of private firms.

The difficulties of the Rwandese refugees in Burundi are mainly the fruit of the poverty of the country and the prevalence of an out-of-work population in the towns. We cannot speak of the conditions of refugees living in the countryside, but it is probable that their condition is even more distressing.

On the other hand, Burundi has embarked on a campaign of national reconciliation and has called back her own refugees who fled before the massacres in 1972. This has political implications, within and without the country, which should be considered: the authorities have no interest in letting it be thought that the Tutsi of Burundi form a single social class with the refugees of Rwanda, and that they stand together against the Hutu who have come home, and every suspicion must be avoided of helping elements hostile to Rwanda, if good relations are to be kept up with the neighbouring state. It should be remembered that Rwanda also gives shelter to refugees from Burundi, and could always encourage them, as an act of reprisal, to threaten the stability of Burundi. In fact, a tacit agreement exists between the two states: 'Keep my people quiet, and I'll look after yours.'

In view of these facts, what solution can be found for this problem? The Rwandese themselves have up to now envisaged two types of solution: there are those who wish to be integrated legally and socially in the country which has received them, while others advocate the return to Rwanda. These two tendencies seem to be merging today, especially since they have become bitterly aware of the tragedy of the Banyarwanda in Uganda: more and more numerous are the Rwandese who seek repatriation. The Rwandese government opposes this obstinately for the reasons we have indicated, which are certainly questionable, but which for the moment are accepted by certain elements of international opinion.

But what country has thrown out part of its population to preserve the other part from economic crisis or from demographic expansion?

Conclusion

Certain conclusions can be drawn from the experience of the Rwandese refugees. We will list a few of them:

1) The problem of refugees in Africa cannot always be resolved by a single state. It has to take account of the relations existing between the host country and the country from which the refugees come, and it is often mixed up with problems caused by the former colonial frontiers, which generally add to the confusion.

2) It seems that frequently, at least at the outset, the refugees tend to settle in the frontier zones, where they find populations with whom they have a certain affinity (of language, culture, etc.). But that does not necessarily reduce the risk of clashes between migrants and natives. The old tribal quarrels can break out at any time and sometimes lead to armed conflicts. And when this occurs, the refugees are those who have the most to lose.

3) When troubles arise which are likely to threaten the stability of the government in power, refugees play the role of scapegoat. It is sufficient to designate 'victims' among those of them who have been able to climb up and take a place in the national bourgeoisie.

4) When there are other immigrants in the country who have the same origin as the refugees, they are rarely spared by the bad feeling. The risk of such an extension of the threat is greater or lesser according to whether the times are times of prosperity or crisis.

5) The economic crisis can increase the hostility to a point where the expulsion of the scapegoats follows naturally. Evidence is supplied by the expulsion of the Rwandese from Uganda, but also, and more recently, by that of the immigrants of Nigeria. Economic immigrants can be potential refugees, as their country is often in no hurry to see them back. It may be necessary to extend the juridical notion of a 'refugee' to include this new category, and to consider the assistance that should be given them.

13. Towards a Better Definition of the Concept of Refugees

Throughout this dossier we have felt the need of a better definition of the term 'refugee', if we are to fight this scourge more effectively. Because we are talking about Africa, let us start from the definition adopted in 1969 by the OAU and show its limitations.

Because of the compromises and the ideological restrictions which were part of the making of this definition, which happens to be the latest one formulated by the OAU, but which is much older, we shall see that these limitations are to be found on two levels:

1) *the level of facts:* because numerous groups of fugitives or expelled persons fail to enter into the definition, although it is incontestable that their situation could be described as that of refugees.

2) *the level of causes:* and here we see the most cruel limitation, as it has the most serious results on our action.

A better definition on the first level, one which would include a greater number of evident facts, would allow stronger and more efficacious action. But this action would remain just a remedy. Take the example of malnutrition. It can be defined as a lack of foodstuffs depriving the organism of a number of products necessary in fixed quantities. With such a definition the victims of malnutrition can be cured. But if we do not know the causes for this lack of foodstuffs, the reasons for which people are deprived of the necessary products, it will be impossible to *anticipate* the scourge and to prevent other persons or groups from being attacked by it. It is the same with the refugees: the reasons and causes indicated in the definition adopted by the OAU are insufficient to the point of allowing no preventive strategy. Who is going to believe that this is pure chance, an inevitability?

The OAU Definition in 1969

The term 'refugee' is applied to any person who, reasonably fearing persecution on account of his race, his religion, his nationality, his membership of a social group or his political opinions, is outside the country of which he has the nationality but cannot, or will not, because of this fear, claim its protection. It also applies to any person who, possessing no nationality and being outside the country in which he had his usual residence because of such events, cannot or will not (because of his fear of persecution) return there.

The term 'refugee' is also applied to any person who, following an aggression, the occupation or exploitation by a foreign power, or other events which seriously disturb public order in a part or the whole of his native country or the country of which he possesses the nationality, is obliged to leave his usual dwelling to seek refuge in another place outside the country of which he is a citizen.

Factual Inadequacies of this Definition

The two paragraphs of the definition have this in common: they consider the tragedy of the refugees as a problem of *persons*. But in reality there are millions of *victims*. This mass phenomenon can only be represented as the displacement of millions of persons by an ideological distortion of juridical terms. And this even more so as the first paragraph speaks of belonging to a race, a religion, a nationality, while in Africa (as in other regions) these connections are first of all seen collectively and quite secondarily as affecting individuals. In most cases the refugees have been menaced or directly persecuted as members of collective groups, and it is as a group that they have escaped (more or less) from the danger.

The first paragraph regards the 'persons' who are already settled outside the country whose nationality they hold and in which they had their usual residence. In the second paragraph the authors of the definition are concerned with what has happened inside the country from which the refugees come. But in neither case is there any mention of populations who have been illegally expelled by the police and the government of the country in question. We now know that a great number of refugees have been so expelled. The latest example is that of two million Ghanaians, living legally in Nigeria and in no way comparable to refugees, which have been expelled *manu militari* by Lagos. These Ghanaians had lived in Nigeria for several years. Of course the definition dates from 1969, but the pogroms in the Ivory Coast against the people of Benin (known as Dahomans at the time) took place in 1958, and the expulsion of the Malians (Sudanese) from Senegal occurred in 1960. There are other examples. According to the two paragraphs of the definition, it is always the refugees who, under the pressure of constraints which we will analyse later, *make the decision* to flee.

What is worse, these fugitives are only considered as refugees if they *cross the frontiers* of the country in which they are citizens or at least regular residents. This fact eliminates from the classification the millions of Black people who, in South Africa, are expelled from their tribal lands and compelled to settle in Bantustans, the 'national frontiers' of which are set up by the White power. And also the inhabitants of villages who, because of the war (especially in the Horn), take refuge in other provinces of the same country, leaving all they possessed behind. These refugees (for that is what they really are) are not officially counted and will have no right to the assistance which the official organizations dole out. If, in 1940, refugees had been defined in the same way, how would they have described the victims of the collapse of the Allied front, fleeing south-wards in France before the advance of the German troops? And yet the borders of European states are rightly regarded as less artificial than those of African countries.

A last limitation of the definition *on the level of facts*, and this seems to us the most serious, is that neither of the two paragraphs makes provision for the case of populations which, having fled from the country of which they are citizens, are refused re-entry by their own government. We have seen that this is now the case for a great number of Rwandese. Here are people who do not come under the definition of refugees if we refer to the criteria of the first paragraph: the impossibility of returning to his country only makes a man a refugee if it is due to *his* way of looking at the situation.

It is evident that such a definition can operate enormous reductions. The only people who will be considered as refugees are those who have decided to cross their national frontiers and judge it too risky to return. The definition succeeds in making the extent of the tragedy less apparent and reduces it to particular or, to say it clearly, exceptional cases. Already ideological distortions become apparent, but they are more on the level of causes than on the level of facts.

Meanwhile, we think it would better fit the facts exposed in this dossier to ask that new elements be included in the definition, so that the term can also be applied to groups (belonging to social categories, tribes, religious communities and/or nationalities) who have been displaced by necessity or by constraint outside their habitual geo-cultural area, be they natives or regular residents, and to which they are unable to return.

Causal Inadequacies

The first paragraph of the OAU definition of 1969 is expressly concerned with refugees *already settled* outside their country, and tries to explain why they neither return to this country nor seek to take advantage of its protection. In other words, this paragraph concentrates more on seeking the reasons for which those 'persons' it considers *remain refugees* than the reasons for their exile. The answer is: *a reasonable fear of persecution* for belonging to a race, a religion, etc.

The expression 'a reasonable fear' is at least equivocal. How can we imagine that thousands of people accept exile and destitution 'unreasonably'? And even if this was the case for some of them, who could be the judge? on what standards? On the other hand it is easy to appreciate the hesitation of those who created the definition: is not simple fear too subjective an element for a text which is to be used to establish the 'rights' of refugees? And would not the mere mention of fear give too great an emphasis to persecution, and so turn the scales too much in favour of the refugees?

And that is all the more true because the motives of persecution enumerated engage directly or indirectly the responsibility of the African governments which had signed the convention from which the definition is taken. In each state the leaders who form the government belong objectively to a race, a religion, a nationality, a social group and a political movement (as there is in all these states a single party). As long as they are in power, these leaders do not belong to the communities which are persecuted or under threat. They affirm that they are at the service of their peoples, who have brought them to power by an almost unanimous vote in free elections. Clearly they have interests in diminishing the risks of persecution, which are presented as uncontrollable blunders or the result of foreign interference. A distinction has to be made between irrational collective manifestations of psychopathy and 'reasonable fear'! Zaire, for example, once through the 'troubles' which helped President Mobutu to come to power, opened its frontiers to the return of its refugees and proclaimed an amnesty to those who feared being persecuted for their political opinions. Why do more than 100,000 Zairese remain in Angola as refugees? It is clearly 'with no reason' that most of them remain in exile, terrified by illusory fear, the source of which is what they have learnt of the fate which met those who did return.

The OAU definition we are studying then establishes, in the category of refugees, a distinction between those who possess the nationality of the country from which they have fled and those who, without possessing that nationality, nevertheless lived there. The first group can be called refugees if they are unable or, because of a 'reasonable fear', unwilling to 'demand the protection of their native country'. Logically, the protection in question should preserve them from brutalities and injuries from the people of the host country. Such a disposition supposes that the consular services of the country from which they have fled are established in the host country, for if these do not exist the refugees are evidently 'unable to ask for their protection'. But where such services exist and possess effective means of action, why do refugees not have recourse to them? Because they fear persecution by these very services! All the evidence points to a context of tribal and/or politico-religious repression. The consular services (or what takes their place) in the host country see to it that the refugees constitute no threat to the regime of the country they represent, and if necessary, they achieve this result by persecution. The OAU definition cannot hide the responsibility of the governments of certain countries with respect to the persecutions to which their refugees are exposed, for these persecutions have the same origin as those they are afraid to encounter if they return to their country.

That is why the definition will be formulated so as to reduce, as much as possible, all reference to such persecutions. Not only must they be 'reasonably feared', but a particular case is made out for each refugee who has simply abandoned his usual residence but does not possess the nationality of the country to which he has fled.

These people, because of 'events' which are not described in detail but which we will try to understand, are supposed to have the greatest difficulty in returning to the country where they habitually reside, because they lack the means or the authorization, or because they are simply afraid. There is a way of interpreting the end of the first paragraph which would make it mean that *only the refugees who do not possess nationality* are unable, or do not wish (because of fear) to return to the country where they usually reside.

The second paragraph contains even more ideological overtones. It no longer concerns refugees already settled outside the country, but all 'persons' obliged to leave the country. It is strange that it be mainly if not only for this second group of refugees that the text details the motives which spur them to leave the country. They have the right to be called refugees on the same grounds as the others, and yet they are distinguished as a group separate from those who precede. That is why it is very important to know whom they are talking about. The formulation of the text can be understood in two different ways, because of a confusion of language:

● If the country where the refugee habitually resides and from which he is fleeing is the same as the country which is suffering from foreign aggression or other troubles, the refugee is in flight under pressure from the events which are taking place on the spot.

● If the refugee has fled the country where he is habitually a resident because *another* country (that of which he is native, or citizen by naturalization) is ravaged by any such aggression or domestic troubles, we can reasonably ask: why should he be fleeing 'to another place', supposedly 'outside the country whose nationality he possesses'?

The distinction may seem specious, but it has serious consequences. In the first case, the refugee has the nationality (by birth or through naturalization) of the country where he resides habitually and from which he is fleeing. In the second case, the refugee is a foreigner in this country, and he takes to exile *because he fears reprisals* as a consequence of troubles affecting the country of which he is a citizen or a native. This is a special case not envisaged in the first paragraph, which must be the reason for the composition of the second.

This seems all the more plausible as we know of facts which correspond to this situation. At Douala, some time after the independence of the Cameroons, the Hausa (who are of Nigerian nationality) living in the New Bell district were persecuted and obliged to flee because of the violence of the Cameroonians. The country had not been attacked from abroad and was not the victim of serious public disorders, but a local riot resulted in the burning of Hausa shops. The causes of this remain obscure, probably linked with the rivalry, in the north of the country, between the Cameroonians and the Nigerians. The consequences took on the character of *reprisals*. The Hausa victims did not generally leave the country, but went to live elsewhere in the Cameroons.

Other cases of this type could be cited, but they seem less frequent than those which correspond to the first interpretation. We can generally agree that the refugees referred to in the second paragraph are those people obliged to leave the country where they usually reside, and in which they have full rights, because their security is indeed threatened by aggression and/or serious troubles (and not only because they have 'reasonable fears' for their security, as the first paragraph would imply).

Here again we are up against ideological bias. The text is drawn up in such a way that the serious troubles only appear as provoked by foreigners or agents from abroad. As to public order, it is assumed to have additional tribal and socio-political value. This is a way of (implicitly!) devaluing struggles waged in the country itself on behalf of national or social freedom from an unendurable 'public order'. Those who drew up the text reveal that they are responsible for, or at least supporters of, such an 'order'.

We may then well ask for a definition of 'refugees' which takes into account, among the causes, the fact that these people are often not only prevented from returning to their country but are also obliged to flee, in order to escape all manner of reprisals and repression threatening their families and the group to which they belong.

The texts that we have just criticized have at least the advantage that they no longer put among the first causes of flight natural calamities or the socio-economic consequences of under-development. They put the accent on the political causes of depopulation, even if in a very insufficient manner and in a resolutely individualistic perspective.

We find the same emphasis in the opening speech of the Conference on the Situation of Refugees in Africa, which was held at Arusha on 7 May 1979. President Nyerere in his analysis defined the refugees as 'people who are now, and perhaps in the future, obliged to flee their fatherland and seek refuge in another country in order to escape persecution, death or famine'. We should remark the order in which he enumerates these dangers. He goes on to describe them as 'victims of racism, of colonialism and of the social changes in Africa', and says they belong to three large groups.

> The first group is composed of political refugees, but the act of giving asylum to these refugees is unhappily not always considered as an humanitarian act . . . The second group contains those who are fighting for liberty, but the United Nations and the other international organizations do not recognize these people as refugees. The third category, which is by far the largest, is made up of men, women and children who are running away from war, from persecution, from religious, racial or cultural conflicts, or from famine and other natural calamities.

117

Part 4:
Resolutions and Projects

14. After the Meeting of 6 November 1982

The extent to which migrations have multiplied in Africa in the last few years, and the fact that some of the exiles come to Europe seeking the status of political refugees, led CIMADE, Education and Liberation, INODEP and the International N'Krumah Movement to look into the problem.

According to statistics furnished by the High Commissioner for Refugees, roughly one refugee out of two in the world comes from Africa, and one in every hundred Africans is a refugee. The question is too often presented from the humanitarian aspect, and this helps to hide the real causes of the exile, and means that the solutions proposed are simply means of assuring their survival.

The associations concerned organized a day of study for 6 November 1982, on the theme: 'Africa has become a land of refugees: what can we do here, what should be done out there?' The aim was first of all to contribute to a better understanding of the situation of refugees and of the relative responsibilities of those who are at the root of their flight, and then to discover what practical actions it would be possible to support to diminish the phenomenon.

The study concentrated on three flashpoints in the continent: (1) the Horn of Africa (Ethiopia, Eritrea, Somalia, Djibouti and Sudan); (2) Central Africa (Zaire, Angola, Rwanda); (3) Southern Africa (South Africa, Zimbabwe, Angola, Mozambique, Lesotho, Botswana). The three regions have different climatic conditions, economic systems and political regimes, but all three produce and receive millions of refugees.

After hearing eye-witnesses from the field, and working together in small groups, the organizers agreed:
a) That if the flight of refugees took different forms in different regions and had different immediate causes, the deep cause common to all its manifestations was to be found on the political level, and for three reasons:
● the refugees flee from anti-democratic and repressive regimes, often under military control;
● wars are kept going by the political strategies of the great powers, and these powers supply the arms to fight them;

● beneath these politico-military problems there are economic interests (sometimes foreign, but also African).

b) That these political causes had been largely determined by the heritage of the colonial age, prolonged in many places by practices and even structures that can be called neo-colonial.

c) That the refugee tragedy could be defined in terms of the widespread violation of the most elementary human rights.

As a consequence, the following measures were proposed:

1) Better information should be available, and it should be better diffused in the international media, with the support of a permanent committee to be set up.

2) Pressure should be applied on all political leaders, including those engaged in the international organizations. Appeals should be prepared and petitions furnished. The action should be co-ordinated with the action of the parties and unions.

3) Support should be organized for groups of refugees and immigrant workers in western countries, as well as for freedom movements in Africa.

4) Development projects should be sponsored and not merely immediate help sent to ensure survival. Their objective should be to help the populations to take their affairs in hand and avoid new catastrophes. They should aim at spreading education and political awareness among the people. These projects should be built up and realized with the help of Africans, especially those who are qualified.

At the end of the day, this communiqué was sent to the press to be published. The limited number of press organs which agreed to publish the information confirms the extent of the task before us.

In accordance with the resolutions made at the closure of the debate, it was decided to set up a permanent committee of information on refugees in Africa. Taking account of the work which has already been done on the subject, three branches are to be established: a permanent committee to co-ordinate all the activities; a documentation centre; and a publication, which is to be the heart of the project and which will diffuse:

● research on the causes of the flow of refugees (analyses and syntheses contributing to this research);

● inquiries into living conditions in the field, life in the refugee camps, efforts made to resettle in countries from which they had fled, descriptions of projects and achievements in health, educational and other fields;

● up-to-date news: politics, what influence the refugees have in political struggles, the evolution of the countries concerned by the problem, as well as news of demonstrations of support, colloquiums, etc. and the results that have already been achieved or which can reasonably be expected.

The aim is to publish strict news accounts and to remain independent of all governmental or supra-national authorities. We also wish to publish data from various governmental or non-governmental organizations which, for various reasons, have not been released.

It is evident that an infrastructure in material and personnel is needed to realize this project. It will have to be financed, and a network must be set up to collect and exchange information coming from Africa.

15. The Second ICARA, held in Geneva, 9–11 July 1984

The Preparation: From Hope to Fear

From 9–11 July 1984 in the Palace of Nations at Geneva the Second International Conference on Assistance to Refugees in Africa (ICARA II) was held. Two of the associations who publish this book were present as observers.

The hopes which could have been vested in this conference diminished progressively *during the stage of its preparation*. The organizers of ICARA II had set the mark high: they wanted to add to the Urgency Assistance voted by ICARA I (in 1981) structures capable of establishing 'durable solutions' to the problems posed by African refugees in Africa. Intergovernmental and governmental associations in Africa and on the international scene had been invited to join with non-governmental organizations and representatives of the refugees themselves to draw up plans for these solutions. Then the 14 African countries which had replied to the invitation of the Secretary General of the UN and submitted proposals were visited, from July 1983, by a team of technical experts from the UN. Most of these countries were situated in Southern or Central Africa or in the Horn.

But the preparatory work of the experts suffered from serious limitations and contradictions. It is an excellent principle to set up 'durable solutions' in harmony with the developmental problems of the countries involved, and the UN HCR insisted strongly on this. The result was a list of 128 projects

> in harmony with the priorities of the national development plans and workable techniques. By order of preference these projects can be classed sectorally in the following way: 28% concern roads, bridges, harbour installations and energy projects; 24% agriculture, silviculture and fisheries; 20% education and training; while 16% were health projects, 10% proposed water supplies, and 2% systems of development and social support.[1]

The same official source affirmed that just the 'expenses for infrastructure' for the entire plan (and not simply the projects in the first sector) would cost US$362 millions. The explanation is clearly given: the experts have succeeded in linking the 'durable solutions' to the development of the *infrastructure* of the countries which host refugees. At this stage of the preliminary work, the organizers of ICARA II cry triumph: this is a world first! 'By introducing the concept that developing the infrastructure is a means to arrive at durable solutions to the refugee problem in Africa, ICARA II will present the broadest long-term approach to the problem of refugees on the African continent that the world has ever undertaken.'[2]

To get to this point, the African government experts and the international experts had worked fairly quickly. Twice, however, the NGOs protested and questioned this 'global method of approach' and the type of analysis it presupposes.[3] But by 30 January the projects were formulated and programmed and their cost estimated.[4] The NGOs, whose contribution 'on the level of information' had been judged important, had nothing further to do than to get down to making the complementary studies of 'practicability', prior to the execution and evaluation of these projects.[5]

None of the preparatory documents of ICARA II that we have been able to consult makes any reference to a 'specific' contribution from the refugees themselves or their representatives in the way of an analysis, an approach to the problem, a 'durable solution', or even a project.

The Conference: A Significant Omission

Before opening the conference, the package was tied up; it had only to survive the discussions. There again, many hopes were dashed. According to custom, the agenda was constructed progressively by consensus. After the provisional agenda of 23 March, a new agenda was presented to the participants for approval, containing a new item: in the haste to get the projects accepted after scarcely three days' work, they had almost forgotten to ask for a reflection on the 'preliminary declarations' (point no. 3) of the UN, the OAU, the UN HCR and the UNPD (UN Programme for Development).

The following elements of these are important:

> On several occasions I have publicly declared how preoccupied I was by the economic and social situation of the African continent. As Secretary General of the UN, I felt it was my duty, at the beginning of this year, to take an initiative to help the international community to understand this situation, and explain that we need to find more resources to support our policies and discover how, by acting together, we can make the efforts of the international community more effective. As you doubtless know, the Economic and Social Council has given the priority, in its Agenda of this summer, to a debate on the economic situation in Africa. I sincerely hope that *this debate* will lead us to establish, according to it a priority of urgency, a framework of action for African problems, among which must be counted the situation of the refugees.[6]

But this debate did not take place, and the participants were not even able to present another approach to the refugee problem. Was that because the institutional framework of the preparation and realization of the conference excluded any discussion of the political dimension of the problem? This does not seem to have been the case, as the same speaker went on to say:

> One of the major tasks of this Conference will be to see how the international community can best cover the financing of these projects. Looking at those which are presented, it seems clear that to put an end to the refugee crisis in Africa and bring things back to normal, different approaches must be used. Voluntary repatriation is of course the best solution, as it goes to the heart of the refugees' dilemma. But that means that the countries in question will have to make proof both of compassion and of political wisdom. I hope that whenever possible individual countries will use their 'good offices' to help restore conditions favourable to the repatriation of the refugees. The principles set out in the Convention of the OAU on Refugees, adopted in 1969, those in the Declaration of Arusha in 1979, and more recently in the Charter of the Rights of Men and Peoples adopted by the OAU are useful and offer a juridical and humanitarian framework for solutions of this type. I cannot stress too strongly that Human Rights should be an essential element of political action.[7]

So either the call for a debate, for different approaches and for reflection on the political aspect was only there 'for form's sake', or there was a contradiction on this last aspect within the preparation for ICARA II. And indeed, just after the Declaration by Mr Perez de Cuellar (the Secretary General of the United Nations), the High Commissioner of the United Nations for Refugees concluded his introductory contribution with these words:

> What is the task which we have to accomplish today?
> We must recognize, in our assistance to the refugees and our support to the countries which receive them, the link between the humanitarian aspects and those which touch development.
> We should then support the programmes which offer the refugees the help of which they have an urgent need and give us new possibilities to find durable solutions (here I am referring to paragraph 5-b of resolution 37/197 of the General Assembly).
> We must also furnish the host countries and the countries in which the refugees are repatriated the help they need to build up their infrastructure (and here I refer to paragraph 5-c of the same resolution).
> Finally we must break new ground and set in motion a process which no single Conference can bring to its conclusion, but which we have the duty, here, to initiate with determination.
> We are going to spend three days in deep debate, *on a basis strictly non-political and humanitarian*. If we talk and act in this spirit, we can be certain that we shall have made a great step forward during this Conference.[8]

Those who had come to the conference hoping to share an analysis of the situation similar to that we have outlined in this book could hope for no solid contribution on these lines.

Towards ICARA III?

Stop Play-acting
What a deception! And the same was felt about other perspectives of ICARA II. The conference only treated the developmental aspect of the problem of African refugees. Even if the conference had been organized by the UN HCR under a development rubric, the representatives of the African countries ought to have taken this exceptional occasion to show that their attitude is more responsible.

The conference became the setting for a scene of begging acted by the African countries, especially those who are the most deeply affected. The absence of the refugees themselves, who were the people principally concerned, was conspicuous, and reveals what a small place they hold in the real preoccupations of African states.

During the intervals, for example, the delegates of Somalia and Ethiopia could be seen talking peacefully in the wings of the conference, as if oblivious of the fact that they are the principal actors in the tragedy.

Or again, certain countries directly involved in the conflicts which swell the ranks of the refugees seem quite happy to go on playing the eternal role of the munificent donor.

For the Africans, this conference should have been an occasion to reflect more deeply on a strategy of reinsertion and see if they are able to accept refugees temporarily or not; and to analyse means of action in many different fields. Among the points which invite new thinking we can quote: Security . . . the rapid distribution of urgent assistance . . . a reduction of administrative red tape which would allow rapid decisions . . . encouraging the refugees to take a part in the administration of their camps . . . requisitioning local services . . . without forgetting ways to prevent new tragedies and the problem of diplomatic mediation.

But the facts leave a bitter taste. The impression left by the delegates' speeches, be they from donor countries or from those who demand, was that everybody's initiative was stifled because they were unable to see the problem other than as a necessary political and economic evil.

The Real Questions
Since 1960, the hinge date of African independence, the whole problem of refugees revolves around the following points:

1) the political unrest awaiting the young nation-states (the putsches are more and more frequent).

2) the chronic lack of a really democratic system in most of the African states.

3) the fact that the industrialized states and the transnational corporations choose to back regimes which are incapable of resolving the fundamental problems of their peoples: self-sufficiency in food supplies; national independence and national sovereignty; and the consolidation of national unity.

4) the continuation of the colonial regime with the regime of apartheid in South Africa causing wars of liberation in Namibia, Angola, Mozambique.

5) the pressure which the great powers put on the weak economies of the young states by means of neo-colonial financial and economic agreements and, in most cases, the imposition of a development geared towards exports.

6) the excessive militarization of the African continent which is progressing rapidly and is maintained by the installation of numerous foreign military bases and the maintenance of Africa in the strategic zones of the great powers with no regard for the African governments. The Horn of Africa has become the biggest arms dump in the continent!

These are the subjects which should have been broached, if only to help define plans of development. Great care was taken to avoid them!

Everyone should understand that we have no *a priori* desire to disparage ICARA II. Our misgivings and our criticism are directed towards the future . . . towards ICARA III, when it is decided to convene this conference. We admit that our analyses are marked by anxiety, notably about the role which will be attributed to the non-governmental organizations if they are invited to collaborate.

At ICARA II only the big charitable organizations or those who were confessional had the right to intervene. The 'small' organizations sat in the balcony during the plenary assemblies. During the work in commissions, which was what interested them most, no translation was provided, and privileged attention was given to the representatives of the richest and best equipped organizations, which made clear their intention of implementing the projects they supported. Is that really the best that the NGOs can offer the international organizations and those which represent the governments?

Could not the HCR have a strong diplomatic force under the control of the UN and the OAU on matters affecting Africa? This would prevent potential conflicts from breaking out, and also stimulate warring governments to negotiate the return of refugees and look after their real reinsertion. The HCR should enjoy sure juridical guarantees and dispose of sufficient financial means to be able to give political refugees with professional aptitudes the opportunity to fit into the society in which they are exiles, using their talents to the full.

We hope that ICARA III will be realistic enough to attack the real problems and that it will get all the actors involved: refugees, African states, NGOs and the different charitable organizations. That would be an effective way to approach the problem and allow the discovery of solutions and remedies capable of relieving the suffering of the African refugees.

Notes

1. United Nations, Service of Information: press communiqué REF/1542, 21 February 1984, p. 2.
2. Ibid.
3. Doc. of 24–25 November 1983 and Correspondance Cimade/HCR/NGOs, April–May 1984.
4. Preparatory working document REF/A/CONF.125/1, dated 25 January 1984.
5. REF/1554 of 6 July 1983, p. 3.
6. REF/1548 dated 9 July 1984, p. 2. Italics added.
7. Ibid., p. 3.
8. Ibid. Italics added.

Conclusion

As we have seen, Africa today enjoys the sad privilege of being 'the continent of refugees': she shelters more than five million of them, that is, half the refugee population of the whole world. This figure represents more than the total population of some states, for example Djibouti, Botswana, Liberia or Gabon, and yet it is growing every day and no solution to the problem appears on the horizon.

There are different reasons for this growth of the refugee population in Africa: inequalities in the distribution of riches and power, the negative attitude of certain African leaders towards any form of criticism, the fact that the well-being of the nation is often mistakenly considered to be that of the chief of state. This in turn leads to a narrow interpretation of what is vital for national security. There is a tendency to define as 'subversive' or 'reflecting foreign influence' any expression of disagreement in society: that is what makes for military governments and states in which only one party is tolerated. Young people are becoming increasingly conscious of the glaring violations of human rights which are perpetrated in Africa. And finally, the superpowers are always meddling in African affairs and foreign ideologies have been imported.

On the other hand, Africa is also well known for the success with which she has repatriated some of the refugees. Since Angola, Mozambique and Zimbabwe have become independent, thousands of refugees have gone back to their country. Today many of them play their part in its development, thanks to the knowledge acquired in the country which hosted them. We are indeed worried about the increasing number of refugees, but we find encouragement in the opportunities which are attracting them to return. The present operation in Djibouti for the repatriation of Ethiopian refugees is for us a sign of hope. Africa certainly has a serious refugee problem to face up to, but there are also a certain number of elements which indicate the way to a solution.

The first of these is the existence of the Organization of African Unity (OAU), which provides a place for African political personalities to tackle delicate and difficult questions such as that of refugees, and look for solutions in the spirit of an African tradition. Doubtless there are still problems to be solved, but the OAU has already succeeded in solving many.

A second positive element is the adoption by the OAU in 1969 of an agreement which lays down the rules for particular aspects of the refugee problem in Africa.

The third element is the explicit affirmation by the agreement that 'giving asylum is a humanitarian and peaceful act . . .' Many people consider this as 'the golden rule', a reflection of the hospitality traditionally extended by Africans to strangers and travellers, and even to fugitives, on the basis of humanitarian feeling.

This is the spirit which has prompted numerous African countries to give a generous welcome to refugees. Thus the Sudan has opened its frontiers to more than 500,000; Djibouti has received more than 30,000; Uganda something like 116,000 and Tanzania near to 160,000; while Angola has admitted a little less than 100,000 and Zaire more than 300,000.

To put this liberal policy into effect, the Africans accept huge sacrifices. When refugees suddenly arrive somewhere, no organizations are ready to receive them; there is only the local community which, in the spirit of African solidarity, shares its poverty and becomes as poor as the refugees themselves. When international assistance arrives (generally a long time after), both the local population and the refugees are in a difficult situation, and sometimes the international aid organizations exclude the local population from assistance on the grounds that they do not need help! Imagine the anguish and the despair that would have been felt if one of the developed countries, with its developed infrastructure, suddenly had to cope with the arrival of 100,000 refugees, let alone 500,000!

Unhappily we have to state that the greater part of the refugees are settled in the least developed countries of Africa, those who are poorly equipped to give help to anybody.

The reality of the African situation is that today, after 30 years of political independence, the economic take-off which we had hoped would better the condition of the masses still remains a dream. A recently published report of the FAO (Organization of the United Nations for Food and Agriculture) points out that 22 African countries are seriously threatened with grave food shortages. According to this report, the assistance in foodstuffs needed by these countries for 1983–84 will amount to 3.2 million tons, and the quantities promised up to now will cover only 19% of this indispensable total. Several of the countries which are in this predicament are hosting refugees. As a matter of fact, the throngs of refugees are quoted here as one of the causes of the food shortage.

More than others, the refugee is at the mercy of circumstances. If he does not meet with people who understand him and offer their affectionate support, if he does not find a social institution to give him counsel or a community to welcome him, he is condemned to death, be it natural death or suicide. Recent examples of these tragedies are numerous. When someone is no longer supported by his customary environment, when the habits and the attitudes which he has so long practised are no longer possible for him, his life depends on his ability to create new structures of behaviour.

What Can WE Do?

After this bird's-eye view of the situation, a fundamental question remains: what is to be done to resolve the problem of the African refugees? We can react to this question in several ways:

1) We can gather information on the extent of the problem of the African refugees and the different elements which are part of it. Is the problem, as some people claim, a purely African affair, or are outside forces involved? Are the problems which exist in Southern Africa and in the Horn of Africa simply created by Africa?

2) Once you have formed your opinion on the basic causes of this situation, talk about it to your friends, the people you live with, the members of the groups in which you are active. Strong public opinion is a powerful instrument capable of working miracles. The independence of Angola and of Mozambique was obtained not only by armed struggle but by the strength of public opinion.

3) Take an interest in the way your country is involved in Africa. How does its policy advance the efforts made to develop Africa? Is this policy controlled by economic or military interests, or by some other type of interest particular to your country? Try to find out all about this and talk about it in your circle of acquaintances.

4) What does your country do to help African refugees, be it by means of intergovernmental organizations or of benevolent institutions? A second international conference on help to refugees in Africa was held in Geneva from 9–11 July 1984. You should encourage churches, action groups and acquaintances to use all their influence to persuade your government to make a generous contribution in response to the appeal of the conference.

5) Analyse carefully the way refugees from Africa are treated in your country and the policy of your government towards them. We do not think it desirable that African refugees should leave Africa in large numbers, but it is evident that most of those who have been able to reach Europe have good reasons for doing so and that they deserve your attention and your philanthropic help.

6) Finally, look carefully at the growing mistrust of foreigners which is to be felt in Europe today. In most cases, the attitude of the wider public towards refugees and, more generally, towards the affairs of Africa is influenced, and even determined, by the way in which these problems are presented in the press and on television. The moment African questions are introduced, bias and excessive simplification are to be observed; this

only adds to the mistrust of foreigners rife among the public and influences their relations with African refugees in Europe.

Attitudes like that result from ignorance. If public opinion is well informed, some prejudices may remain, but no deep antipathy. We hope that this book will have contributed somewhat to spreading such information.

Melaku Kifle
World Council of Churches

Appendixes

1. African Charter on Human and Peoples' Rights

Preamble

The African States members of the Organization of African Unity, parties to the present convention entitled 'African Charter on Human and Peoples' Rights',

Recalling Decision 115 (XVI) of the Assembly of Heads of State and Government at its Sixteenth Ordinary Session held in Monrovia, Liberia, from 17 to 20 July 1979 on the preparation of a 'preliminary draft on an African Charter on Human and Peoples' Rights providing *inter alia* for the establishment of bodies to promote and protect human and peoples' rights';

Considering the Charter of the Organization of African Unity, which stipulates that 'freedom, equality, justice and dignity are essential objectives for the achievement of the legitimate aspirations of the African peoples';

Reaffirming the pledge they solemnly made in Article 2 of the said Charter to eradicate all forms of colonialism from Africa, to coordinate and intensify their cooperation and efforts to achieve a better life for the peoples of Africa and to promote international cooperation having due regard to the Charter of the United Nations and the Universal Declaration of Human Rights;

Taking into consideration the virtues of their historical tradition and the values of African civilization which should inspire and characterize their reflection on the concept of human and peoples' rights;

Recognizing on the one hand, that fundamental human rights stem from the attributes of human beings, which justifies their national and international protection and on the other hand that the reality and respect of the people's rights should necessarily guarantee human rights.

Considering that the enjoyment of rights and freedoms also implies the performance of duties on the part of everyone;

Convinced that it is henceforth essential to pay a particular attention to the right to development and that civil and political rights cannot be dissociated from economic, social and cultural rights in their conception as well as universality and that the satisfaction of economic, social and cultural rights is a guarantee for the enjoyment of civil and political rights;

Conscious of their duty to achieve the total liberation of Africa, the peoples of which are still struggling for their dignity and genuine independence, and undertaking to eliminate colonialism, neo-colonialism, apartheid, zionism and to dismantle aggressive foreign military bases and all forms of discrimination, particularly those based on race, ethnic group, color, sex, language, religion or political opinions.

Reaffirming their adherence to the principles of human and peoples' rights and freedoms contained in the declarations, conventions and other instruments adopted by the Organization of African Unity, the Movement of Non-Aligned Countries and the United Nations;

Firmly convinced of their duty to promote and protect human and peoples' rights and freedoms taking into account the importance traditionally attached to these rights and freedoms in Africa;

Have agreed as follows:

Part I: Rights and Duties

Chapter 1 — Human and Peoples' Rights

Article 1
The Member States of the Organization of African Unity parties to the present Charter shall recognize the rights, duties and freedoms enshrined in this Charter and shall undertake to adopt legislative or other measures to give effect to them.

Article 2
Every individual shall be entitled to the enjoyment of the rights and freedoms recognized and guaranteed in the present Charter without distinction of any kind such as race, ethnic group, color, sex, language, religion, political or any other opinion, national and social origin, fortune, birth or other status.

Article 3
1. Every individual shall be equal before the law.
2. Every individual shall be entitled to equal protection of the law.

Article 4
Human beings are inviolable. Every human being shall be entitled to respect for his life and the integrity of his person. No one may be arbitrarily deprived of this right.

Article 5
Every individual shall have the right to the respect of the dignity inherent in a human being and to the recognition of his legal status. All forms of exploitation and degradation of man particularly slavery, slave trade, torture, cruel, inhuman or degrading punishment and treatment shall be prohibited.

Article 6
Every individual shall have the right to liberty and to the security of his person. No one may be deprived of his freedom except for reasons and conditions previously laid down by law. In particular, no one may be arbitrarily arrested or detained.

Article 7
1. Every individual shall have the right to have his cause heard. This comprises:
    (a) the right to an appeal to competent national organs against acts of violating his fundamental rights as recognized and guaranteed by conventions, laws, regulations and customs in force;
    (b) the right to be presumed innocent until proved guilty by a competent court or tribunal;
    (c) the right to defence, including the right to be defended by counsel of his choice;

(d) the right to be tried within a reasonable time by an impartial court or tribunal.

2. No one may be condemned for an act or omission which did not constitute a legally punishable offence at the time it was committed. No penalty may be inflicted for an offence for which no provision was made at the time it was committed. Punishment is personal and can be imposed only on the offender.

Article 8

Freedom of conscience, the profession and free practice of religion shall be guaranteed. No one may, subject to law and order, be subjected to measures restricting the exercise of these freedoms.

Article 9

1. Every individual shall have the right to receive information.
2. Every individual shall have the right to express and disseminate his opinions within the law.

Article 10

1. Every individual shall have the right to free association provided that he abides by the law.
2. Subject to the obligation of solidarity provided for in Article 29 no one may be compelled to join an association.

Article 11

Every individual shall have the right to assemble freely with others. The exercise of this right shall be subject only to necessary restrictions provided for by law in particular those enacted in the interest of national security, the safety, health, ethics and rights and freedoms of others.

Article 12

1. Every individual shall have the right to freedom of movement and residence within the borders of a State provided he abides by the law.
2. Every individual shall have the right to leave any country including his own, and to return to his country. This right may only be subject to restrictions, provided for by law for the protection of national security, law and order, public health or morality.
3. Every individual shall have the right, when persecuted, to seek and obtain asylum in other countries in accordance with laws of those countries and international conventions.
4. A non-national legally admitted in a territory of a State party to the present Charter, may only be expelled from it by virtue of a decision taken in accordance with the law.
5. The mass expulsion of non-nationals shall be prohibited. Mass expulsion shall be that which is aimed at national, racial, ethnic or religious groups.

Article 13

1. Every citizen shall have the right to participate freely in the government of his country, either directly or through freely chosen representatives in accordance with the provisions of the law.
2. Every citizen shall have the right of equal access to the public service of his country.
3. Every individual shall have the right of access to public property and services in strict equality of all persons before the law.

Article 14
The right to property shall be guaranteed. It may only be encroached upon in the interest of public need or in the general interest of the community and in accordance with the provisions of appropriate laws.

Article 15
Every individual shall have the right to work under equitable and satisfactory conditions, and shall receive equal pay for equal work.

Article 16
1. Every individual shall have the right to enjoy the best attainable state of physical and mental health.
2. States party to the present Charter shall take the necessary measures to protect the health of their people and to ensure that they receive medical attention when they are sick.

Article 17
1. Every individual shall have the right to education.
2. Every individual may freely take part in the cultural life of his community.
3. The promotion and protection of morals and traditional values recognized by the community shall be the duty of the State.

Article 18
1. The family shall be the natural unit and basis of society. It shall be protected by the State which shall take care of its physical and moral health.
2. The State shall have the duty to assist the family which is the custodian of morals and traditional values recognized by the community.
3. The State shall ensure the elimination of every discrimination against women and also ensure the protection of the rights of the woman and the child as stipulated in international declarations and conventions.
4. The aged and the disabled shall also have the right to special measures of protection in keeping with their physical or moral needs.

Article 19
All peoples shall be equal; they shall enjoy the same respect and shall have the same rights. Nothing shall justify the domination of a people by another.

Article 20
1. All peoples shall have the right to existence. They shall have the unquestionable and inalienable right to self-determination. They shall freely determine their political status and shall pursue their economic and social development according to the policy they have freely chosen.
2. Colonized or oppressed peoples shall have the right to free themselves from the bonds of domination by resorting to any means recognized by the international community.
3. All peoples shall have the right to the assistance of the States party to the present Charter in their liberation struggle against foreign domination, be it political, economic or cultural.

Article 21
1. All peoples shall freely dispose of their wealth and natural resources. This right shall be exercised in the exclusive interest of the people. In no case shall a people be deprived of it.

2. In case of spoliation the dispossessed people shall have the right to the lawful recovery of its property as well as to an adequate compensation.

3. The free disposal of wealth and natural resources shall be exercised without prejudice to the obligation of promoting international economic cooperation based on mutual respect, equitable exchange and the principles of international law.

4. States party to the present Charter shall individually and collectively exercise the right to free disposal of their wealth and natural resources with a view to strengthening African unity and solidarity.

5. States party to the present Charter shall undertake to eliminate all forms of foreign economic exploitation particularly that practised by international mono-polies so as to enable their peoples to fully benefit from the advantages derived from their national resources.

Article 22

1. All peoples shall have the right to their economic, social and cultural develop-ment with due regard to their freedom and identity and in the equal enjoyment of the common heritage of mankind.

2. States shall have the duty, individually or collectively, to ensure the exercise of the right to development.

Article 23

1. All peoples shall have the right to national and international peace and security. The principles of solidarity and friendly relations implicitly affirmed by the Charter of the United Nations and reaffirmed by that of the Organization of African Unity shall govern relations between States.

2. For the purpose of strengthening peace, solidarity and friendly relations, States party to the present Charter shall ensure that:

    (a) any individual enjoying the right of asylum under Article 12 of the present Charter shall not engage in subversive activities against his country of origin or any other State party to the present Charter;

    (b) their territories shall not be used as bases for subversive or terrorist activities against the people of any other State party to the present Charter.

Article 24

All peoples shall have the right to a general satisfactory environment favorable to their development.

Article 25

States party to the present Charter shall have the duty to promote and ensure through teaching, education and publication, the respect of the rights and free-doms contained in the present Charter and to see to it that these freedoms and rights as well as corresponding obligations and duties are understood.

Article 26

States party to the present Charter shall have the duty to guarantee the independence of the Courts and shall allow the establishment and improvement of appropriate national institutions entrusted with the promotion and protection of the rights and freedoms guaranteed by the present Charter.

2. The Burden Should Be Better Distributed

Speech to Conference on Refugees in Africa: Arusha, 7 May 1979, by President Nyerere

Mr Chairman, Your Excellencies, Ladies and Gentlemen,
First, it is my pleasant duty to welcome to Tanzania all the delegates to this conference, and all those from other countries who will assist the conference in its work — not forgetting the interpreters. We hope that you find in this conference centre all that you need for efficient work, and that you find in Arusha and elsewhere in Tanzania all that you need for a pleasant stay in our country.

This Conference is about people: about the prospects, and indeed the very life, of people who are now, or may in the future be, forced to flee from their homelands and seek refuge in another country in order to escape persecution, or death, or starvation. There are now about 3.5 million such refugees in Africa. Nine African countries have a smaller population than that. All these men, women and children are Africans for whom the governments and liberation movements represented in this conference are severally, and through the OAU jointly, responsible.

Thus, if our claim to speak for Africa has any meaning, then these 3.5 million people are our responsibility. This conference has to face up to the implications of our common humanity with these millions of souls. They are victims of forces beyond their control; it could happen to any of us. The manner in which they now unavoidably look to us for succour may be the way we ourselves will tomorrow be looking to others.

Refugees for one day or for a lifetime

But we have to be realistic and hard-headed about this problem of refugees. We have, in particular, to recognize that it is not getting smaller. In 1967 there were less than three-quarters of a million refugees in Africa; in 1977 alone, 700,000 new refugees crossed the borders of Africa. 1979 does not appear so far to be reversing the upward trend, despite some recent very welcome repatriations of those whom changed circumstances or policies have allowed a safe return to their homes.

This conference has to deal with a continuing problem and one which will not just go away by itself if we do nothing. Even if there was not a single new refugee in Africa from this day forward, it is relevant to remember that a refugee stays a refugee for up to 70 years if we do not make provision for his or her integration into our societies. Either we make arrangements whereby refugees can become self-

142

supporting, or they have to be fed for a lifetime by the sweat of the rest of Africa's people. Our work at this conference is of long-term importance — or it should be.

Yet I want to emphasise that this conference is about people, not about things, or cattle. Refugees have only one thing in common — that they have fled from their country. Even the cause of their flight will be different. It may be persecution, or social upheaval, or war, or it may be famine which causes a disregard of borders. The refugees are usually, but not quite always, without property or means of earning a living. But apart from the fact of seeking refuge they are as varied as Africa's people are varied. They will be of many ideologies or of none, of many different religions, and many different cultures. They may be nomadic or pastoral, just as they may be agriculturalists or urban workers. They will have different levels of education; they will be different in ambition, and in character. All refugees are certainly victims, but they do not consequently lose their individual ideas about life and their own purpose. They will include the ambitious, the optimist, the pessimist, the honest hard-working man and the sly delinquent; the person who will make the best of things, and the man who will grumble about everything. And so on. Generalizations about refugees are very dangerous; all that can safely be said is that they have sought refuge.

Further, a particular host country may at different times, or even simultaneously, have different and antagonistic waves of refugees from a neighbouring country which is going through a long period of social and political disturbance. Yet all refugees are individuals with a right to life in Africa. All need a chance to recreate their lives in Africa, and to regain the dignity of being self-reliant and making a contribution to the development of our continent.

A heavy burden

But it is not only the refugees and the circumstances of their flight which differ. So do the conditions and the circumstances of the countries to which the refugees flee. All are poor countries — that is as much as can be said. A few — like Tanzania — have areas of under-utilized land on which refugees can be settled if there is an investment of capital. But this is unlikely to be the most productive land, and in some countries — like Djibouti or Algeria — it will be waterless desert requiring at least very heavy investment in irrigation schemes. And some countries have no spare land at all; Burundi and Rwanda are already so over-populated by nationals that they need to find opportunities for emigration. And while professionally trained refugees can — perhaps after language courses — be found useful work, the unskilled urban refugee creates a big problem for countries already at their wits' end to deal with urban unemployment.

Yet refugees are in no position to consider the problems of the country they flee to. And fortunately our independent states have not had to bear the whole burden alone. The United Nations High Commissioner for Refugees, and the Voluntary Agencies, have given and continue to give tremendous help to any African government which appeals for assistance and is willing to co-operate with them. We in Tanzania have found these bodies helpful as regards the initial problem of providing food, medical supplies, etc., as a matter of emergency relief. We have also found them willing and able to help in the planning and execution of long-term re-settlement schemes. Indeed, in this country we have a number of rural settlement schemes which have now, through the co-operation of the government, the UNHCR and Voluntary Agencies, become self-reliant communities, producing their own food and selling cash crops sufficient to meet their other expenses. In some cases these refugee settlements have already been passed over to the government for normal administration on the same terms as other villages and development schemes of the country.

I would like therefore to use this opportunity to pay tribute to the office of the High Commissioner for Refugees, and to the personnel and supporters of the religious and other charitable voluntary agencies which have assisted my country in this work for Africa's people. Without their investment of capital, and their skilled and professional personnel, we would not have been able properly to meet our responsibilities to these victims of racism, colonialism and social change in Africa. And in paying this tribute I do not believe that I do so only on behalf of Tanzania; the reports submitted to the various United Nations committees show clearly that Tanzania's experience with these organizations has been shared by all other African countries which face this problem and which try to deal with it.

An African problem

But although this external help has proved vital, I repeat: the refugees of Africa are primarily an African problem, and an African responsibility. This has been fully acknowledged by the OAU which has called upon all its members to accede to the UN Convention of 1951 and the UN Protocol of 1967. Thirty-three African states have done so out of an OAU membership of 46. The OAU has also drawn up, and adopted at the Heads of State and Government meeting in 1969, its own OAU Convention on Refugees.

This OAU Convention recognizes the need for a humanitarian approach to the problems of refugees, and sets out the basic rights and duties, both of the refugees and of the receiving states. In particular — and this is very important to peace in Africa — the Convention states clearly that, 'The grant of asylum is a peaceful and humanitarian act and shall not be regarded as an unfriendly act by any Member State.' Further, it acknowledges that no person should be compulsorily or forcibly returned by an African state to the territory he has left and where his physical integrity or liberty would be threatened. At the same time, the OAU Convention excludes acts of subversion by refugees against the territory they have left, and exempts criminals from the protection of refugee status.

This Convention should be the basis of legal, social and economic provision for refugees in our continent. It was adopted and signed by 41 heads of government and state at the 1969 Addis Ababa meeting. Yet only 18 nations of Africa have ratified it. And ten years have passed.

Political refugees, freedom fighters and persecuted populations

The OAU Convention was the indirect product of the very serious and useful Conference on Legal, Economic and Social Aspects of African Refugee Problems, which was held in October 1967. That conference discussed the refugees under three principal categories. First, the political refugees, who are mostly urban dwellers, and to a greater or lesser extent educated people. At that time it was envisaged that most of these would come from the parts of Africa still dominated by colonialists or racialists, and it is still true that many of such people are from South Africa, Rhodesia or Namibia. But the political and social upheavals in free Africa have now also contributed to the numbers of political refugees, and unfortunately it is not always the case that giving refuge to such people is accepted as 'not being an unfriendly act'. My own country has experience of this, and of the pressures which can be applied by other African states calling upon a host nation either to repatriate particular refugees forcibly or at least to withdraw their permission to stay.

The second category of people recognized is the freedom fighters, who are in a special position. The OAU recognizes their right to pursue the struggle for libera-tion, and the right of the host country to aid them with the full approval and support of the OAU if its government so decides. Thus freedom fighters need to be distinguished from other refugees, for the United Nations and other international bodies do not recognize them as refugees at all. And their needs are different; this conference can appropriately leave this matter to the OAU Liberation Committee.

The third category of refugees is by far the most numerous. It consists of men, women and children fleeing from war, from racial, religious, or cultural persecu-tion or conflict, and from famine or other natural disasters. For a minority of these refugees the problem from which they are fleeing is a temporary one; sometimes it is only a matter of a few weeks until they can go home. But although virtually all refugees initially expect to return home at some time, there will very often be large numbers of people who will be unable to return home safely for months or years to come. It is impossible to deal with these refugees as if all that is required is temporary relief from distress. They must as quickly as possible be given a means of producing or earning their own livelihood. The only practical way of proceeding is to work as if they are likely to be permanent inhabitants of their host state. Investment to meet their needs will never be wasted in the growing African economies even if these refugees should all in the future return to the place from whence they came. For repatriation does take place; for example some 70,000 Mozambican refugees returned from Tanzania to their homeland after the Portuguese colonialists were defeated.

Neither refoulement nor privileges

The 1967 Conference discussed the problems and needs of these different groups of refugees at various times. For there is always the immediate need for emergency aid. Then there is the onward movement, or long-term aspect of their rehabilitation.

About the immediate problem there is very little which can usefully be said — but there is a lot which has to be done. People arrive in their hundreds or thousands, hungry, thirsty, without shelter, and with no more possessions than they can carry on their back. They have to be fed, housed and provided with emergency medical needs if epidemics (which would also affect the local popula-tion) are to be avoided.

In Africa, some of the rural or small town refugees are on occasions able to take refuge with their kin, at least in the first instance, because our borders cut across traditional tribal groupings. Indeed, it is reported that in countries like Cameroon and Gabon, where refugees from Equatorial Guinea have entered in large numbers, this type of settlement has become long-term and dominant. It should not be assumed, however, that it is therefore without cost to the host government.

Improved and expanded schools, health and other public services are required, in addition to specific arrangements for these families who have no kin or who for other reasons cannot be locally integrated.

The medium and long-term settlement of refugees does, however, raise many points of principle and of policy. Perhaps the most basic among these is that while refugees need special help if they are to re-establish their lives and to be integrated among the population of the host country, they must not be given a privileged position, with greater services and a better standard of living than the local inhabitants — who may be very poor indeed. The UNHCR has recognized this; so has the OAU. It is for this reason that we in Tanzania have been able to develop, in cooperation with the UN and Voluntary Agencies, area settlement schemes which deal with the special needs of the refugees and at the same time uplift the productive capacity and the social provisions for all the people living nearby.

A better distribution among African countries

But settlement in the country of first refuge is not always possible. Countries like Botswana and Lesotho, for example, cannot possibly absorb all those who flee to them from Rhodesia and South Africa. Onward movement has to be organized. And then the question arises — movement to where?

The 1967 conference acknowledged the need for the refugee burden of Africa to be shared with some concept of equality among all African states. It has not happened yet. Thus, at the end of 1977 Mozambique had about 70,000 refugees — apart from the freedom fighters — of whom one quarter were under 14 years of age. Tanzania has currently about 200,000 refugees; Zaire and Angola still have even larger numbers despite recent organized repatriations. But some countries — particularly those in West and North Africa (except for Algeria) — have only one or two hundred refugees. Is it impossible for something to be done about this disparity — either for some of the less affected states to provide rural refugee settlements or for them at least to contribute to the heavy local costs involved for the countries which do give such hospitality?

The Addis Ababa Conference of 1967 made a large number of recommendations also, especially concerning the kind of legislation which would safeguard the social and economic rights of refugees while taking full account of the problems and needs of local people. It made suggestions about the vexed problem of the right to work; it set down guidelines related to the land settlement of refugees and the development of integrated settlements which would benefit both the refugees and the local population. Further, there was in 1967 a discussion, and some indication of a possible way forward about the problem of travel documents for refugees and how this could be dealt with on an African basis — a matter of great importance to countries like Botswana and Swaziland. There were proposals also for an 'African Bureau' under the auspices of the OAU, which could help cooperation among African states over refugee problems. It was suggested that this could act as a clearing house to coordinate scholarship needs and offers, at the same time as helping qualified refugees to get jobs in Africa rather than — as at present — expensive expatriate personnel being recruited to fill needs for which no citizen is available. Indeed, most of the subjects on the agenda of this conference were the subject of discussion and recommendation in 1967.

Your conference should therefore be considering Africa's experience in the light of the earlier debates and of what has been done over the last twelve years. And certainly, since 1967 many countries have done a very good job in coping with large-scale new influxes of refugees, giving them somewhere to stay and food to eat. Some countries have made progress in developing integrated settlement schemes; some have been generous with scholarships for refugees from Southern Africa. In all these cases there will be some experience which can help this conference to deal with the continuing problem.

In addition, there has been general acceptance of the principle of 'non-refoulement', which precludes the returning of any refugee to the country from which he is fleeing or has fled. Unfortunately, however, this principle has been broken by some countries on certain occasions — with subsequent and to be expected death of the refugees returned. Where criminal acts are involved, and a just legal system exists, this principle does not apply. But when a tyrant demands a refugee on the grounds that he or she is a criminal, there is no justification in humanity for surrendering the person to him. Nor, when a refugee offends against the laws or security of a host country, is there any excuse for returning him to countries like Smith's Rhodesia, apartheid South Africa, or Amin's Uganda. The accused should either be dealt with inside the host country, or expelled to another refuge with the help of the High Commissioner for Refugees. I hope that this conference will reaffirm Africa's commitment to the principle of 'non-refoulement'; it is a basic humanitarian law. These results from the 1967 conference have been important. But there were other recommendations.

I do not know how many African nations have amended their legislation where necessary, or already have satisfactory laws governing the rights and status of refugees. But I doubt if the figure is large, and I do know that we in Tanzania have not made any changes. In any case, it is certain that this meeting cannot be told anything very much about progress in sharing the burden which refugees cause for some nations. And I am not aware either that there has been any concerted or coordinated African action to deal with the question of travel documents — although again, some countries do a very great deal unilaterally on this matter.

And education? At what point do refugee children become eligible for secondary or technical education on the same basis as nationals — or do they remain aliens for ever? Which countries have carried out the OAU Council of Ministers' recommendation that refugees should not be charged the economic school or college fees? Which countries have even worked out a coherent policy on these things, let alone implemented it? And so on. Honest reporting on all these subjects of discussion in 1967 are likely to be depressing.

Five loaves and two fishes

Why is this? I do not believe it is a result of ill will, but rather that all the governments of Africa are busy, and hard pressed, trying daily to perform the miracle of the five loaves and two fishes. They are subject to many pressures from their people and on behalf of economic interests elsewhere. And there is no countervailing pressure in support of the refugee victims of injustice and oppression. The only pressure is our own awareness of Africa's unity and of our common humanity with our brothers and sisters. It appears that this is not a very strong pressure in comparison with others to which we are subject.

But there is a further problem — the problem of bureaucratic organization. In most of our countries the Ministry of Foreign Affairs deals with matters connected with international organizations and the OAU. The Home Ministry deals with refugee matters inside the country. A Ministry of Lands has to be involved in any land settlement, an Education Ministry for matters related to schools or school fees, and Regional Authorities on integration with local people, and so on. It needs a major effort if young and poor countries are to overcome the resulting problem of organization and coordination, and to ensure that refugee policy is clearly worked out and then efficiently implemented.

At OAU level also there is the problem of too much to do and too few resources with which to do it. Heads of Government meetings, and even Foreign Ministers' meetings, usually go on long into the night, and still many important issues are not adequately considered. And when a decision is made, there remains the question of its implementation. Individual states do not always carry out agreements reached with and by the representatives at OAU meetings.

Mr Chairman, I have talked for a long time. And it may be that I have not been very diplomatic. But this is not because I am unconcerned with the matters you will be discussing. It is because I am concerned, and because I am hoping that if we recognize what is, then we shall be able to get on with the work of making what is into what should be.

Our resources are very limited, and the demands made upon us are very large. But I do not believe that dealing with the problems of 3.5 million people, and giving them a chance to rebuild their dignity and their lives, is an impossible task for 46 nations and their 350 million inhabitants.

Your Excellencies; you have my good wishes for your conference, and for your success in translating its decisions into action by Africa's governments.

Thank you.

3. The High Commission is Disturbed by the Renewal of Armed Attacks on Refugee Camps[1]

Geneva. The Executive Committee of the High Commission of the United Nations for Refugees (HCR), assembled since 10 October, seems to be finding the greatest difficulty in obtaining a consensus to adopt a proposal for a 'declaration forbidding military or armed attacks against the camps of refugees or zones where they are settled'. The High Commission is disturbed by the military or paramilitary attacks made on refugee camps in Africa, in Latin America or in Asia, and so much so that it has devoted a supplement of more than forty pages of its monthly review *Refugees* to the subject, under the title: 'Stop the massacres!'

The editorial, signed by Léon Davico, head of the information service of the HCR, begins with the following paragraph:

> *It is certainly not much fun to be a refugee in a camp, whether you are enclosed by barbed wire or not. If, as well, you are threatened, sometimes night and day, with attacks by armed men, threatened with extortion, with aerial bombardments or piratical incursions, it becomes unbearable. A camp, even a town, to say nothing of being out at sea, can become a rat trap, a way of the cross, a tomb.*

In Southern Africa, this publication reminds us, planes scatter death among the refugees. In the China Sea, those who have taken to the sea continue to suffer the attacks of pirates. In Indochina, whole divisions launch deadly attacks on refugee camps. In Central America, armed 'civilians' cross frontiers in helicopters to attack them.

Annick Billard, the Chief Editor of the publication, recalls that in October 1981 the Executive Committee, aware of the *'need to take special measures to protect these refugees and guarantee their security'*, had entrusted the ambassador of Switzerland, Mr Felix Schnyder, with the task of making a report on the different aspects of this tragic situation. The series of large-scale massacres started on 4 May 1978, when the South African air force bombarded the camp of Namibian refugees at Kassinga (Angola), killing 600 people and leaving 400 wounded. Since then, the attacks have been repeated all over the place.

Mr Schnyder's report stresses the fact that such acts constitute a violation of the sovereignty of the host country. The governments of these countries have the duty not only to protect their own territory, but also the camps and zones in which refugees are settled. The task of the HCR is made more difficult by the fact that its competence is purely humanitarian, but the fact that it is charged to ensure the international protection of refugees necessarily sets political problems.

According to Mr Schnyder the host country should ensure, if it wants to avoid giving pretexts for intervention, that the refugees do not indulge in any action which might risk provoking such attacks. He also recommends that the HCR have

149

regular and unimpeded access to the camps and zones of settlement, and that these be as far as possible from the frontier.

The proposal of the declaration which is now under fire is aimed at no country in particular and at no special form of political regime. It limits its affirmations to the fact that *'when a State gives asylum to refugees it accomplishes a pacific and humanitarian act'*, and deplores and condemns *'the growing frequency and extent of attacks made on camps and zones of settlement for refugees'*. It *'recognizes that military training or armed exercises practised in such camps or zones, as well as the utilization of situations arising from the presence of refugees, or even the use of the refugees themselves for military or political ends, can often expose them to serious physical dangers'*. The text concludes with an appeal to all states to *'conform strictly'* to the terms of the declaration, which aims at *'forbidding military or armed attacks against the camps of refugees'*.

Isabelle Vichniac

Note

1. Published in *Le Monde*, 19 October 1983.

4. The Refugees and the Food Problem in Africa

The two main problems in Africa are the problem of refugees and the shortage of foodstuffs. Is there a link between the two? To insist on finding a binding link between the lack of food and depopulation would be an unwarranted exercise. Rather would it be true to say that there is a series of interactions between the two facts which tend to make both of them more serious and to push further into the future the discovery of solutions.

Let us see why there are so many refugees in Africa and if the problem of the scarcity of food can be considered as one of the causes.

Most of them have left the region in which they lived because of wars, civil wars, or wars for national freedom. There are also cases where part of the population is running away from cruel dictatorships. We had examples of this until very recently in Uganda and Zimbabwe, and now there is Equatorial Guinea, and Somalia where we see the conflicts of Ogaden and Eritrea. The reasons for all these movements of the population are above all political.

But we must admit that flights resulting from economic causes have already taken place in Africa, and that in these cases they have a direct link with the food situation. A first example was the terrible drought in the Sahel, a second the rush to the towns (Dakar, Bamako . . .), or into camps where it was only possible to nourish them because of international food aid. In both cases we find the problem of food at both ends of the chain.

We can define the second case as structural, the first being accidental. Here shortage is evidently the first reason why they move. It is generally true that the problems of the farmers nourish (if we may risk this metaphor!) a continuous movement from the country towards the town. The poor living conditions in the country, the disdain in which most public authorities hold the villager, the unduly heavy taxes levied on what are at the outset only small incomes, are in part at least the origin of a veritable haemorrhage of the productive agricultural forces towards the towns, where jobs are not easy to find and living conditions are risky.

In this case a chain of causes among which the impoverishment of the country, the extroversion of the African peoples, the dependency in which they find themselves with respect to the industrial powers, and the economic policies of states which favour an urban style of development, is the origin of what we call an economic depopulation and the crowding in peri-urban areas of a special type of refugee: populations undergoing urbanization.

The problem is all the more serious because the rapid growth of towns is today a major obstacle to a well-balanced development of the territory. Certain African capitals are inhabited by a fifth of the total population of the state and almost all who dwell in towns: they are completely ungovernable.

The movement of the population sometimes goes farther, either from one country to another (from Upper Volta, for example, to the Ivory Coast or to Ghana), or from Africa to the industrialized countries.

Be the refugees economic or political, they create another problem which has serious consequences: in certain regions which have been deserted by their inhabitants, all cultivation has become impossible because of the lack of man-power: there are no hands to till the soil. This was the case last year in Uganda, where in several regions the seed was not sown.

That is how, in many regions of Africa, depopulation engenders famine, which in its turn accelerates depopulation. Progressively irreversible movements to abandon the countryside are created. And as the depopulation of the countryside is not offset by an increase in productivity, the total production of foodstuffs by the country does not increase as fast as the population. At best it remains constant, thus increasing the dependency of the young state on foreign supplies.

In the host countries (Somalia, for example), the refugees are not often producers and they do nothing to offset the burden they put on the shoulders of the active rural population, unless a major appeal is made to international help as is often the case.

Food aid is easier to receive when there are refugees. There are even some countries, like Somalia, who inflate the number of refugees they receive so as to receive more assistance. But the assistance sent is not just of any type. They receive cereals, oleaginous plants, particularly soya beans, and milk products.

These are distributed free to the governments by the USA and the EEC. The local governments sell them a little cheaper than local produce. It is thus hoped to work a change in the people's eating habits so that it will later be possible to sell them the excess products of America and the European Community.

Who makes something out of this assistance?

In the countries which receive it, it benefits those people who live in the towns. In this way the governments keep people quiet and avoid social unrest. The profits from the sales go to pay the civil servants (they were intended to be used to advance development projects), while the army and the police receive ration tickets. On the whole this helps the balance of payments for the countries who profit from it.

In the countries which send it, the EEC uses it as a means of regulating their excess production and avoiding high storage costs. For the USA it is an outlet to dispose of the by-products of cattle feed. The soya oil is exported to Latin America and North Africa, and the cattle feed to Europe, where they feed the cows which are going to produce an excess of milk to be sent to Africa under the assistance programmes. Assistance also serves as a field of experimentation for new food products, and it is a competitive factor because, as we have seen, it captures the urban markets from the local producers. African towns no longer depend on their rural producers for their food supply, but on food assistance programmes from abroad; an abnormal situation indeed!

So if the refugee problem does not necessarily create a situation of food shortage, it makes things worse in the sense that the balance between the producers and the non-producers is inverted in favour of the non-producers, with no compensation on the level of the growth of productivity. In some African countries the situation has reached the point where not only the rural population is unable to nourish a constantly growing town population, but it is becoming less and less able to meet its own needs.

Are there any solutions in view?

It is clear that the problem of political refugees needs another type of solution than those which will meet economic needs. The case of rural depopulation is again quite different and involves the choice of a type of development. It is an illusion to imagine that rural depopulation can be stopped: it is far too advanced and its political and economic causes are too considerable for it to be possible to reverse the tendency. But the African states must imperatively slow it down if they do not want to engender an imbalance with catastrophic results.

This is necessary because the problems in the towns are now beyond measure, and also because the industrial countries are tending to seal their frontiers and will do so more and more. The excess manpower has no future in the towns and must find its living in the countryside.

If the economic choices are modified, the depopulation can be slowed down. We should cease to favour a development for export which is based on a western model quite unsuited to the circumstances. We should give African farmers the technical and financial means to increase their productivity and their revenues without making them marginal. And that means ceasing to see African development on an industrial model, implying techniques which need a lot of capital and very little manpower.

All the efforts made to modernize the rural situation, especially by introducing mechanization, should take account of the human factor.

It is only at the price of heartrending revisions of our economic policies that we shall be able to increase the production of foodstuffs in Africa, stopping the desertion of the country areas and bettering the living conditions of their inhabitants.

Sophie Bessis

5. Refugees in Africa

	1981	1986[1]
Algeria	151,000	167,000
Angola	73,000	92,000
Botswana	1,000	5,000
Burundi	200,000	250,000
Cameroons	265,000	13,000
Central African Republic	7,000	42,000
Congo	—	1,000
Djibouti	42,000	25,000
Egypt	5,000	5,500
Ethiopia	60,000	11,000
Gabon	30,000	—
Ghana	250	—
Ivory Coast	—	600
Kenya	3,500	8,000
Lesotho	10,000	11,500
Morocco	500	—
Mozambique	100	1,000
Nigeria	105,000	5,000
Rwanda	10,150	50,000
Senegal	5,000	5,200
Somalia	1,300,000	700,000
Sudan	438,000	1,000,000
Swaziland	6,000	8,000
Tanzania	140,000	180,000
Togo	—	1,800
Uganda	112,400	180,000
Zaire	400,000	317,000
Zambia	36,000	96,000
Zimbabwe	—	46,000

1 Unconfirmed figures, compiled from those of various NGOs.
Table shows numbers of refugees *in* each country.

Index

THE VANISHING FOREST
THE HUMAN CONSEQUENCES OF DEFORESTATION

A REPORT FOR THE INDEPENDENT COMMISSION ON INTERNATIONAL HUMANITARIAN ISSUES

This new report for this top-level international commission highlights the rapid destruction of the world's remaining tropical rainforests.

Some two percent of these forests are being destroyed or degraded every year. In South America, West Africa and South East Asia, the remaining forests can no longer be assumed to be an automatically renewable resource. This Report stresses the devastating consequences for the people of these areas as loggers, dambuilders and ranchers take over the forests from their indigenous inhabitants.

But there are other consequences that affect all humanity. This Report argues that deforestation is destroying a natural resource that is *the* long-term economic base of the planet. Even more seriously, it is jeopardising the planet's life-support systems — as deforestation threatens irreversible climatic changes and losses of the gene pools we require for future agricultural and medical progress.

There is an alternative. Sound environmental management of the world's forests is possible. What we need — and urgently before the accelerating scale of destruction makes it too late — are policy changes that make forest conversion a vehicle of sustainable development so that human civilisation in the tropics can continue, *and* that preserve those forest areas of particular ecological value.

128pp Tables
Hb 0 86232 631 1   £9.95 $14.95
Pb 0 86232 632 X   £3.95 $6.95

Current Affairs ● Environment

THE ENCROACHING DESERT
THE HUMAN CONSEQUENCES OF DESERTIFICATION

A REPORT FOR THE INDEPENDENT COMMISSION ON INTERNATIONAL HUMANITARIAN ISSUES

Following on the publication of their first report, *Famine: A Man-made Disaster?* (Pan, 1984), this new report for a top-level international commission focusses attention on the relentless spreading of the world's deserts.

More and more fertile land is being turned into barren wasteland — not just in the Sahel, but in other areas like the high Andes and parts of India. 230 million people are now at risk. What are the causes? What are the human consequences? What was wrong with the Plan of Action which the UN Conference on Desertification set up in 1977? And why has it not been implemented?

The consultants who have drawn up this disturbing Report make clear the shortcomings on the part of Third World governments, Western donors, and the multilateral agencies. They draw on information from every part of the world to make the case for urgent action now. For this Report is not defeatist. It points to examples of effective remedial action — in China, Syria, Niger — and sets out the policies required if the climate of our entire planet is not to be put seriously at risk by accelerating desertification.

128pp Tables
Hb 0 86232 633 8   £9.95 $14.95
Pb 0 86232 634 6   £3.95 $6.95

Current Affairs ● Environment

BINA AGARWAL

COLD HEARTHS AND BARREN SLOPES
THE WOODFUEL CRISIS IN THE THIRD WORLD

The world's *other* energy crisis — rapidly shrinking supplies of the wood and charcoal on which most Third World peasants and urban poor still depend for fuel — is the subject of this scholarly and comprehensive book. Drawing evidence from all parts of the world, Dr Agarwal analyses the scale of the problem, its complex causes, and its consequences for both the ecologies and agricultural systems of countries, and for individual users. She explains why the solutions sought — afforestation schemes, more efficient wood-burning stoves, biogas plants and solar cookers — have failed, and argues that technical innovations are not enough. What is required is a political context that enables users (the poor, and women especially) to participate in their design and dissemination.

This book is a significant contribution to the literature on renewable energy, afforestation and rural development; it will be of value to a broad cross-section of policy-makers, programme initiators and scholars.

Dr Agarwal is an Associate Professor at the Institute of Economic Growth, Delhi. Educated at Cambridge and Delhi Universities, she has been a Visiting Fellow at the IDS, Sussex, and is the author of *Mechanisation in Indian Agriculture* (1983) and has contributed to *World Development*, the *Journal of Peasant Studies*, and *Economic and Political Weekly*.

240pp Tables Bibliography Index
Hb 0 86232 539 0   £18.95 $29.95
Pb 0 86232 540 4   £6.95 $10.95
Not for sale in India and the USA

Environment ● Development Studies

BARRY MUNSLOW (EDITOR)

AFRICA: PROBLEMS IN THE TRANSITION TO SOCIALISM

This book offers a succession of profound analyses of the strategies former liberation movements have pursued once in power, and the obstacles they have encountered in their attempts to break radically with prevailing neo-colonial patterns. It explores why they have found it so difficult to transform the forces of production inherited from their colonial and capitalist pasts, and to meet the people's essential needs.

Basil Davidson examines the contrasting experiences of the Cape Verde Islands and Guinea Bissau. Dr Bhagavan uses unpublished economic information to portray the present crisis of Angola's economy. Bertil Egero investigates Mozambique and the difficulties its democratic innovations have faced. More general issues are also raised. Robin Cohen explores how far Marxism has put down roots in Africa while Ben Turok examines the present state of the Left. Bie Nio Ong looks at the position of women and Barry Munslow discusses the general determinants shaping progressive African countries' diverse attempts at socialist transition.

Barry Munslow has written extensively on questions of socialist transition in Africa. He is the author of *Mozambique: The Revolution and Its Origins* and edited *Samora Machel: An African Revolutionary: Selected Speeches and Writings.* He is a member of the Editorial Working Group of the *Review of African Political Economy.*

272pp Bibliography Index
Hb 0 86232 427 0   £18.95 $29.95
Pb 0 86232 428 9   £6.95 $10.95

Africa ● Current Affairs ● Political Economy

CHIBUZO NWOKE

THIRD WORLD MINERALS AND GLOBAL PRICING: A NEW THEORY

This study examines the distribution of the enormous wealth inherent in the Third World's mineral resources. Dr Nwoke criticises the bargaining model usually used to explain relations between global corporations and Third World governments. Instead he develops the Marxist theory of ground rent to argue that today's mineral crisis lies in the struggle between Western mining companies and the Third World over which side can appropriate most 'rent' from international mining. Only if the Third World can realize the full surplus profit available, can it maximize its producer power. Supported by evidence from all over the world, Dr Nwoke's book constitutes a major theoretical advance, as well as having significant political implications.

"Nwoke's extension of Marx's rent theory to the sphere of mining is original, enlightening and explicated with clarity. It helps make sense of OPEC and similar phenomena, and thereby speaks directly to the political options that are open to us." Immanuel Wallerstein

Dr Nwoke is a Research Fellow with the Nigerian Institute of International Affairs. He holds a doctorate from the University of Denver. His articles have appeared in *Monthly Review*, *Africa Today*, and *Review: A Journal of the Fernand Braudel Center*.

272pp Tables Bibliography Index
Hb 0 86232 441 6   £18.95 $29.95
Pb 0 86232 442 4   £6.95 $10.95

Political Economy ● Development Studies

ANN SEIDMAN

MONEY, BANKING AND PUBLIC FINANCE IN AFRICA

This textbook is designed for economics students and those already working in banks, public financial institutions and planning. Its comprehensive treatment assembles information from all parts of the Continent, while concentrating on the very diverse experiences of Nigeria, Tanzania and Zimbabwe.

Monetary and fiscal questions are dealt with in the context of the practical development problems caused Africa by the impact of the world capitalist system. These questions include control of the banking system, appropriate tax policies, how to raise capital, debt management, and relations with the transnational commercial banks as well as the IMF and World Bank.

Professor Seidman supplements conventional economic analysis with a radical approach critical of its assumptions and perspectives. She also analyses the planning, budgetary and banking experiences of socialist countries in Eastern Europe and Asia so that the advantages and pitfalls inherent in their attempts to chart an independent economic course may become better known.

Professor Ann Seidman is a distinguished economist who has taught in many different African countries, including Ghana, Tanzania and Zimbabwe, as well as holding appointments at various U.S. universities. She is the author of eleven books on development strategy, planning and multinational corporations in Africa.

384pp Tables Charts Bibliography Index
Hb 0 86232 429 7   £22.95 $35.95
Pb 0 86232 430 0   £8.95 $13.95

Political Economy